Speaking and LISTENING

Activities to cover all areas of oral language

What do sea monsters live on?

fish and ships!

where? when?

who? what do you think?

why? what?

Janna Tiearney

6250UK REV: 02/07

Chestnuts Primary School
Black Boy Lane
LONDON, N15 3AS
Tel: 020 8800 2362
Fax: 020 8880 1372
email: office@chestnuts.haringey.sch.uk

SPEAKING AND LISTENING *(Lower)*

Published by Prim-Ed Publishing 2005
Copyright© Janna Tiearney 2005
ISBN 978-1-92096-224-1
PR–6250

Additional titles available in this series:
SPEAKING AND LISTENING *(Middle)*
SPEAKING AND LISTENING *(Upper)*

This master may only be reproduced by the original purchaser for use with their class(es). The publisher prohibits the loaning or onselling of this master for the purposes of reproduction.

Copyright Notice

Blackline masters or copy masters are published and sold with a limited copyright. This copyright allows publishers to provide teachers and schools with a wide range of learning activities without copyright being breached. This limited copyright allows the purchaser to make sufficient copies for use within their own education institution. The copyright is not transferable, nor can it be onsold. Following these instructions is not essential but will ensure that you, as the purchaser, have evidence of legal ownership to the copyright if inspection occurs.

For your added protection in the case of copyright inspection, please complete the form below. Retain this form, the complete original document and the invoice or receipt as proof of purchase.

Name of Purchaser:

Date of Purchase:

Supplier:

School Order# (if applicable):

Signature of Purchaser:

Offices in: United Kingdom: PO Box 2840, Coventry, CV6 5ZY **Email:** sales@prim-ed.com
Australia: PO Box 332, Greenwood, Western Australia, 6924 **Email:** mail@ricgroup.com.au
Republic of Ireland: Bosheen, New Ross, Co. Wexford, Ireland **Email:** sales@prim-ed.com
R.I.C. Asia: 5th Floor, Gotanda Mikado Building, 2–5–8 Hiratsuka,
Shinagawa-Ku Tokyo, Japan 142–0051 **Email:** elt@ricpublications.com

Internet websites
In some cases, websites or specific URLs may be recommended. While these are checked and rechecked at the time of publication, the publisher has no control over any subsequent changes which may be made to webpages. It is *strongly* recommended that the class teacher checks *all* URLs before allowing students to access them.

View all pages online

http://www.prim-ed.com

FOREWORD

Speaking and listening forms an integral part of a child's education. Our main means of communicating with the world is through speaking.

Children of today generally spend hours being passively entertained by TV and computer games. Therefore, it is vital that during their time at school, children acquire skills in speaking and listening and practise them in a variety of situations.

Obtaining these skills means not only do children learn to converse more freely, but hopefully they will gain confidence in speaking so that they can communicate more effectively; for example, in giving their own point of view, giving instructions, requesting information, giving a speech, discussing topics with peers, having conversations, talking about personal experiences and telling jokes.

The books in this series are:
- *Speaking and listening – Lower (Ages 5–7)*
- *Speaking and listening – Middle (Ages 7–9)*
- *Speaking and listening – Upper (Ages 9–11)*

CONTENTS

Teacher notes .... iv–v	Your project *(worksheets)* 46–47	Act it out! *(teacher page)* 92
Curriculum links .... vi–vii	Children's meals *(teacher page)* 45	Act it out! *(worksheets)* 94–95
Assessment proforma ix	Children's meals *(worksheets)* 48–49	Set the scene *(teacher page)* 93
Make it better *(teacher page)* 2	Writing for yourself *(teacher page)* 50	Set the scene *(worksheets)* 96–97
Make it better *(worksheets)* 4–5	Writing for yourself *(worksheets)* 52–53	Silly stuff! *(teacher page)* 98
Tell them what to do! *(teacher page)* 3	Do not disturb! *(teacher page)* 51	Silly stuff! *(worksheets)* 100–101
Tell them what to do! *(worksheets)* 6–7	Do not disturb! *(worksheets)* 54–55	Happy hour *(teacher page)* 99
Noisy! *(teacher page)* 8	School in the past *(teacher page)* 56	Happy hour *(worksheets)* 102–103
Noisy! *(worksheets)* 10–11	School in the past *(worksheets)* 58–59	Clap! *(teacher page)* 104
You're giving it away! *(teacher page)* 9	Tell them all about it! *(teacher page)* 57	Clap! *(worksheets)* 106–107
You're giving it away! *(worksheets)* 12–13	Tell them all about it! *(worksheets)* 60–61	That's nonsense! *(teacher page)* 105
Talking without speaking *(teacher page)* 14	Give all the details! *(teacher page)* 62	That's nonsense! *(worksheets)* 108–109
Talking without speaking *(worksheets)* ... 16–17	Give all the details! *(worksheets)* 64–65	Listen! *(teacher page)* 110
Mime it! *(teacher page)* 15	Ask it! *(teacher page)* 63	Listen! *(worksheets)* 112–113
Mime it! *(worksheets)* 18–19	Ask it! *(worksheets)* 66–67	Sounds *(teacher page)* 111
Read together! *(teacher page)* 20	What's your opinion? *(teacher page)* 68	Sounds *(worksheets)* 114–115
Read together! *(worksheets)* 22–23	What's your opinion? *(worksheets)* 70–71	What would happen if ...? *(teacher page)* .. 116
Make it right! *(teacher page)* 21	What is it like to be a teacher? *(teacher page)* ... 69	What would happen if ...? *(worksheets)* 118–119
Make it right! *(worksheets)* 24–25	What is it like to be a teacher? *(worksheets)* 72–73	Read this! *(teacher page)* 117
Past and future *(teacher page)* 26	Yesterday *(teacher page)* 74	Read this! *(worksheets)* 120–121
Past and future *(worksheets)* 28–29	Yesterday *(worksheets)* 76–77	Old favourites *(teacher page)* 122
It's not nice! *(teacher page)* 27	Read a book *(teacher page)* 75	Old favourites *(worksheets)* 124–125
It's not nice! *(worksheets)* 30–31	Read a book *(worksheets)* 78–79	About your book *(teacher page)* 123
Order! *(teacher page)* 32	Can you remember? *(teacher page)* 80	About your book *(worksheets)* 126–127
Order! *(worksheets)* 34–35	Can you remember? *(worksheets)* 82–83	What experience did you have? *(teacher page)* 128
What did we talk about? *(teacher page)* 33	How do you feel? *(teacher page)* 81	What experience did you have? *(worksheets)* 130–131
What did we talk about? *(worksheets)* ... 36–37	How do you feel? *(worksheets)* 84–85	Sense it! *(teacher page)* 129
Summer fun! *(teacher page)* 38	Tell a story *(teacher page)* 86	Sense it! *(worksheets)* 132–133
Summer fun! *(worksheets)* 40–41	Tell a story *(worksheets)* 88–89	Music *(teacher page)* 134
How do you do? *(teacher page)* 39	Reading is fun! *(teacher page)* 87	Music *(worksheets)* 135–136
How do you do? *(worksheets)* 42–43	Reading is fun! *(worksheets)* 90–91	
Your project *(teacher page)* 44		

Prim-Ed Publishing   www.prim-ed.com

SPEAKING AND LISTENING   iii

Speaking and listening – Lower provides a wide range of activities to develop children's oral language skills. Each activity consists of two pages of worksheets and one page of accompanying teacher notes.

TEACHER PAGE

A teacher page accompanies each pair of children's worksheets. It provides the following information:

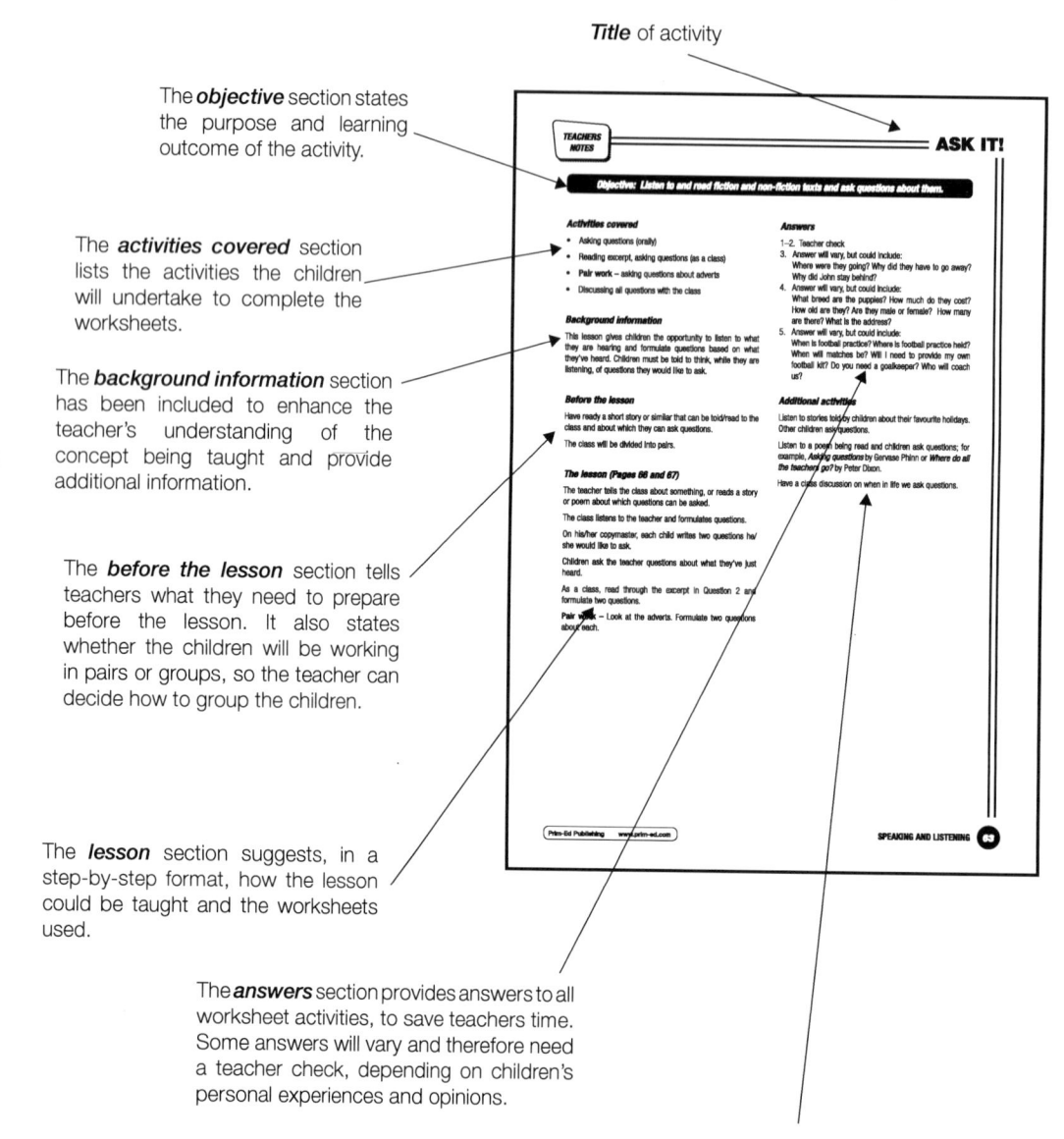

Title of activity

The **objective** section states the purpose and learning outcome of the activity.

The **activities covered** section lists the activities the children will undertake to complete the worksheets.

The **background information** section has been included to enhance the teacher's understanding of the concept being taught and provide additional information.

The **before the lesson** section tells teachers what they need to prepare before the lesson. It also states whether the children will be working in pairs or groups, so the teacher can decide how to group the children.

The **lesson** section suggests, in a step-by-step format, how the lesson could be taught and the worksheets used.

The **answers** section provides answers to all worksheet activities, to save teachers time. Some answers will vary and therefore need a teacher check, depending on children's personal experiences and opinions.

The **additional activities** section can be used to further develop the objectives being taught, as consolidation or extension. Suggestions for suitable websites are sometimes included, to enhance and combine language and ICT learning. Suggestions for stories and poems for children to listen to, read aloud and/or discuss, are also sometimes provided.

SPEAKING AND LISTENING

Prim-Ed Publishing   www.prim-ed.com

TEACHERS NOTES

CHILDREN'S WORKSHEETS

Each page of teachers notes is followed by two worksheets for children to complete. A variety of worksheets are provided, which may require children to read, discuss, answer questions, write, draw, record thoughts or opinions, follow instructions etc.

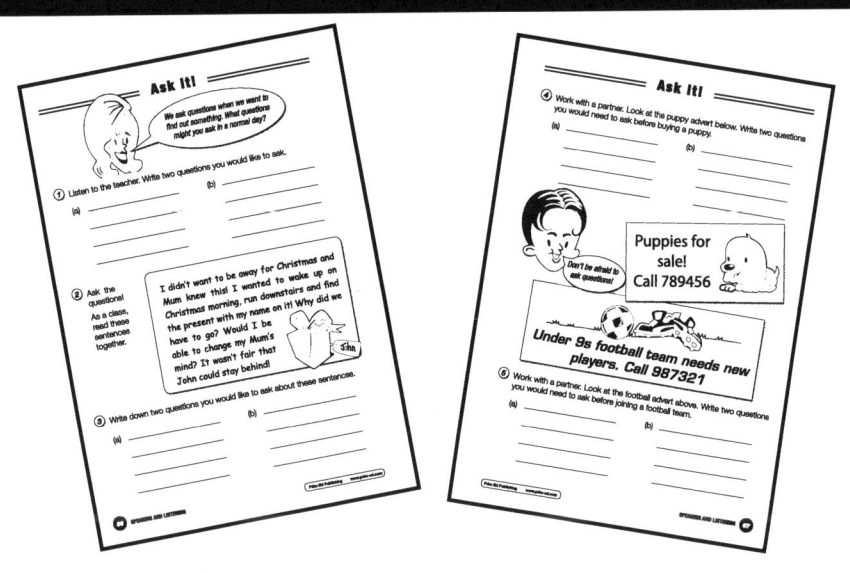

ADDITIONAL TEACHER INFORMATION

There is much group work, pair work and class work in these lessons. Teachers should not feel daunted by this. Even though it is a speaking and listening lesson, there must be structure to it. Guidelines need to be given to children as to what they can and cannot do. During group work and pair work, teachers should walk around, assisting where necessary. If a teacher thinks it is necessary, a group leader can be appointed. Change these positions from time to time. Children should be moved around in pairs or in groups so they get to communicate with children they have not had much contact with. Teachers can explain to children that this will happen from time to time and children should not show dissatisfaction when placed with others – there will be times when they can be with their friends. The teacher should decide who will make up the pairs/groups before the lesson begins.

Some allowance has to be made for less able children, or children who are extremely shy. The teacher should, in such cases, be encouraging and try to involve the child in the activity. There are also children who are very confident about speaking out loud, and such children could dominate activities. This should be gently discouraged!

The teacher is obviously the best person to set the example of how we should communicate orally. Teachers should, in most cases, correct children when they use slang or an incorrect word, but the teacher should always approach this in a friendly and sensitive manner.

As the lessons are photocopiable, a suggestion is that all speaking and listening worksheets be kept in a folder, or children could have their own 'speaking and listening portfolio'. Then, at the end of the year, it can be clearly seen what oral language has been covered and there won't be worksheets lying all over the place.

A few websites have been included. Although these have been checked, the teacher should check again before using them. There is a large number of great websites that would enhance many of these lessons and teachers should make use of them with their children.

Interesting facts are also included on many of the worksheets.

Suggestions for poetry, mostly humorous poetry, have been provided. Obviously, poetry is not always funny, but at this level we don't want children becoming afraid of poetry. Rather, we want them enjoying and understanding it. Teachers must use their discretion about extra reading for the lessons, and use whatever they think will best suit their class.

Some teachers may feel a little uneasy about teaching speaking and listening as it is a lesson of talking, something we are always telling children not to do! The teacher has the ability to set the correct tone for the lesson, and provided guidelines have been explained to the children, there should be no problems. If lessons are going to be particularly noisy, there is no harm in taking the lesson to the playground, if the weather permits! Speaking and listening lessons should be lessons that both the teacher and children look forward to.

Have fun!

CURRICULUM LINKS

Country	Subject	Level	Objective
England	English (Speaking and listening)	KS 1	• Speak clearly, fluently and confidently to different people. • Speak during different activities, in different contexts and for different purposes. • Listen, understand and respond to others. • Listen to each other, adults and recordings. • Interact with groups and join in group discussions. • Interact with groups for a range of purposes. • Participate in a range of drama activities. • Use features of spoken standard English. • Know how speech varies in different circumstances and to take into account different listeners.
		Yr 1	• Describe incidents or tell stories from their own experience. • Listen with sustained concentration. • Ask and answer questions and make relevant contributions. • Explore familiar themes and characters through improvisation and role-play. • Retell stories, ordering events using story language. • Listen to and follow instructions accurately. • Take turns to speak, listen to suggestions and talk about what they are going to do. • Act out own and well-known stories, using different voices for characters. • Interpret a text by reading aloud with some variety in pace and emphasis. • Explain their views to others in a small group and decide how to report the group's views to the class. • Discuss why they like a performance.
		Yr 2	• Speak with clarity and use intonation when reading and reciting texts. • Listen to others, ask relevant questions and follow instructions. • Listen to views and preferences of others, agree steps to take and identify contributions by each group member. • Adopt appropriate roles in groups and consider alternative courses of action. • Tell real and imagined stories using conventions of familiar story language. • Respond to presentations by repeating some highlights and commenting constructively. • Ensure everyone contributes, allocates tasks, consider alternatives and reach agreement. • Consider how mood and atmosphere are created in recorded performance. • Use language and gesture to support explanations. • Listen to a talk by an adult, remember some specific points and identify what they have learned. • Work effectively in groups by ensuring each group member takes a turn, challenging, supporting and moving on. • Present parts of traditional stories, own stories or work from different parts of the curriculum for members of their class.
Northern Ireland	English (Talking and listening)	KS 1	• Have opportunities, arising from classroom and first-hand experience, to develop their talking and listening in a variety of contexts. • Talk to a wide range of audiences. • Engage in talking and listening for a variety of purposes; for example, conversations, discussions, telling stories, talking about events, asking/answering questions, giving instructions and explanations, talking about their work and expressing thoughts, feelings and opinions. • Engage in a range of talking and listening activities. • Express their thoughts and feelings. • Present ideas and information. • Take turns at talking and listening. • Share and co-operate in pairs or group activities. • Think about what they say and how they say it. • Read aloud, inflecting appropriately, to emphasise the meaning of what is read. • Use appropriate quality of speech and voice, speaking audibly and clearly. • Discuss features of language. • Be aware of the implications of purpose and audience.

CURRICULUM LINKS

Country	Subject	Level	Objective
Scotland	English (Listening, watching and talking)	A	• Listen to and discuss a range of texts. • Convey information to a variety of other people. • Interact in small groups and engage in purposeful talk. • Talk about stories, class activities and events at home and school. • Be aware of listeners and speak clearly and audibly. • Evaluate and improve their performance at talking.
		B	• Listen to and discuss a range of texts, giving and justifying preferences. • Experience rhyme and rhythm. • Convey more complex information to a variety of people, showing awareness of audience needs, sequence of essential details and clarity and calmness of delivery. • Engage in a wider range of group activities with structured situations for developing talk. • Show an awareness of others and the need to take turns when working in groups. • Value the contributions of other group members. • Explore their own feelings and experiences and those of others. • Reflect through mime and role-play. • Be aware of listeners and speak clearly and audibly. • Evaluate and improve their performance at talking.
Wales	English (Oracy)	KS 1	• Talk for a range of purposes. • Consider how talk is influenced by the purpose and by the intended audience. • Listen carefully and show understanding of what they see and hear. • Participate in drama activities and improvisations. • Respond to drama they have watched and participated in. • Recognise the importance of language that is clear, fluent and interesting. • Speak with confidence, making themselves clear, organising what they say and choosing words with precision. • Incorporate relevant detail in explanations, descriptions and narratives. • Use the conventions of discussion and conversation. • Listen with growing attention and concentration, so they can respond appropriately and ask and answer questions that clarify their understanding. • Relate their contributions in a discussion to what has gone before and take different views into account. • Consider their own speech and how they communicate with others, particularly in more formal situations or with unfamiliar adults. • Develop confidence in their ability to adapt what they say to their listeners and to the circumstances, recognising how the language differs. • Extend their vocabulary through activities that encourage their interest in words. • Speak with clear diction and appropriate intonation. • Understand the importance of standard English.

Speaking and listening assessment proforma

Name

Class

Date

Curriculum strand

Curriculum objective

Task(s)

The child was asked to:

Assessment

The child:	Demonstrated	Needs further opportunity

Teacher comment

MAKE IT BETTER

TEACHERS NOTES

Objective: Experience challenging vocabulary and sentence structure from the teacher.

Activities covered

- Discussing slang words
- Improving sentences (as a class)
- **Pair work** – having conversation using slang words/no slang words

Background information

Listening to the teacher using vocabulary and correct sentence structure is an ongoing process. The teacher should, in most cases, correct informal language, and be aware of using correct language himself/herself! The teacher should 'sneak in' more difficult vocabulary on a constant basis and encourage children to find out what the words mean.

Children should have a wordbook, set out in alphabetical order, where they can write all new words they learn. This book can then be referred to and these new words used to enhance their writing. This lesson focuses on improving sentences.

Before the lesson

Have sentences ready for improving orally as a class. For example, 'I'm gonna lie down', could be 'I am exhausted after a long day, I think I will take a nap'.

I'm gonna tell on ya!/Ring me Mum and tell her to fetch me, OK?/Shut up!/You better eat them veggies! Examples of other slang words: bloke (man), grub (food), lolly (money), cop (police officer), yeah (yes), freak out (get angry), dough (money), munch (eat), spin (drive), graft (work), mate (friend), telly (television), craic (fun), mutt (dog), footie (football) etc.

The class will be divided into pairs.

The lesson (Pages 4 and 5)

Have a class discussion about slang. Get the children to come up with slang words and words that are not formal English. Each time a slang word is used, replace it with formal English. The teacher writes the slang words and the formal version of them on the board.

As a class, improve the sentences on the copymaster. Children fill in the better sentence of their choice.

Children write one sentence about themselves, and then write it again, using better words.

Pair work – Children have a conversation using slang words as much as possible (looking at the board for ideas).

Children have the same type of conversation using no slang at all! (Set a time limit for each conversation; for example, 3 minutes.) Conversations can be about anything; for example, last holiday, their school, their homework, a TV programme.

Answers

1. (a) That shirt is not to my taste./What an awful shirt./I do not like that shirt.
   (b) The teacher is angry with me.
   (c) The children were fooling around in class.
   (d) This book is not to my taste./I did not enjoy this book./This is not my kind of book.
   (e) Please go away!/Please leave me alone./Please let me be.
   (f) I want to go out.
   (g) I prefer hot dogs to hamburgers.

2–3. Teacher check

Additional activities

The same type of lesson can be completed with sentence structure. The children will be presented with sentences where the word order is clumsy and inappropriate. Working as a class, these sentences can be improved.

Read more challenging poetry.

Watch sections of cartoons/children's TV programmes and listen for any slang.

Teachers can get ideas from websites, but many of these 'slang' websites have adult content, so they are not suitable for children. Look at *www.peevish.co.uk/slang*

Have a classroom display with slang words and what the formal form of the words is; for example: wanna = want to, fab = fabulous.

Look at slang words which are specific to the children's own country or local area.

Have a 'slang-free' day.

SPEAKING AND LISTENING

TEACHERS NOTES

TELL THEM WHAT TO DO!

Objective: Listen to stories, descriptions, instructions and directions and respond to them.

Activities covered

- Discussing instructions and directions – when do we use them?
- Following teacher's instructions
- **Pair work** – describing objects while other draws
- **Pair work** – giving and following directions on a grid

Background information

Children are practising this in their everyday lives. This lesson gives them more practice in giving clear directions and also listening carefully to instructions given by others.

Before the lesson

The class must be divided into pairs. Have ready a list of oral instructions to give the children.

The lesson (Pages 6 and 7)

Start the lesson with a discussion on when we have to listen to instructions and when we might need to give instructions; for example, giving someone directions to get somewhere, taking down homework, doing chores for parents, building a model, completing a task like a project, entering competitions.

The class must stand and carry out verbal instructions. Move at quite a fast pace so that children have to concentrate on what you are saying; for example, touch your left ear with your right hand, put your hands on top of your head, rub your nose with your left thumb, pat your tummy with both your hands, take two little jumps, touch your right knee with your right hand, put your left hand behind your back, close your left eye, stretch your arms right up, give a big smile and clap your hands!

Children must get into pairs. On the copymaster, each child describes something (an object) to his/her partner, who must draw while listening to the description. Children will then swap.

Pair work – Each child chooses a particular animal on the grid that he/she want his/her partner to land on. The child must give instructions as to how to get there. Words to be used: left, right, up, down, diagonal. (Make sure children know the meaning of diagonal.)

Answers

Teacher check

Additional activities

Children give directions to their home from the school, and their partner must repeat the instructions.

Children give clear and precise instructions, orally, on how to perform a task; for example: feed the cat, brush their teeth.

Listen to a short story told by the teacher and answer questions about it.

Listen to poetry being read and answer questions orally about the details; for example, *My room* by Steve Turner, *Parents like you to* by Gervase Phinn (looking at instructions parents and teachers give us), *Our head teacher* by Brian Moses (looking at descriptions).

Children can bring road maps to school and discuss them with their partners.

Children can look at a map of a city centre and follow instructions from the teacher on how to get somewhere.

Make it better

*Sometimes we use slang words when we are speaking or writing; for example, **'I'm gonna call ya'** instead of **'I'm going to call you'**.*

1 Rewrite these sentences. Make your sentences better!

(a) What a gross shirt!	
(b) The teacher is mad with me!	
(c) The kids were messin' in class.	
(d) This book is stupid.	
(e) Buzz off!	
(f) I wanna go out.	
(g) Hamburgers are OK but hot dogs are yummy.	

4 SPEAKING AND LISTENING   Prim-Ed Publishing   www.prim-ed.com

Make it better

2 (a) Write one sentence about yourself.

_____

_____

(b) Now rewrite it, using better words!

_____

_____

3 (a) Have a conversation with your partner. Try to use as many slang words as possible!

I am fab!

The first word spoken on the moon was 'okay'!

(b) Now have the same conversation using no slang at all!

(c) Which conversation sounded better?   1st ☐   2nd ☐

Remember! Try not to use too much slang in your writing and speaking!

Prim-Ed Publishing   www.prim-ed.com   SPEAKING AND LISTENING   5

Tell them what to do!

Can you follow instructions?

1 (a) Draw the object that your partner is describing.

(b) What have you drawn? _____

(c) Were you correct? yes   no

6 SPEAKING AND LISTENING   Prim-Ed Publishing   www.prim-ed.com

Tell them what to do!

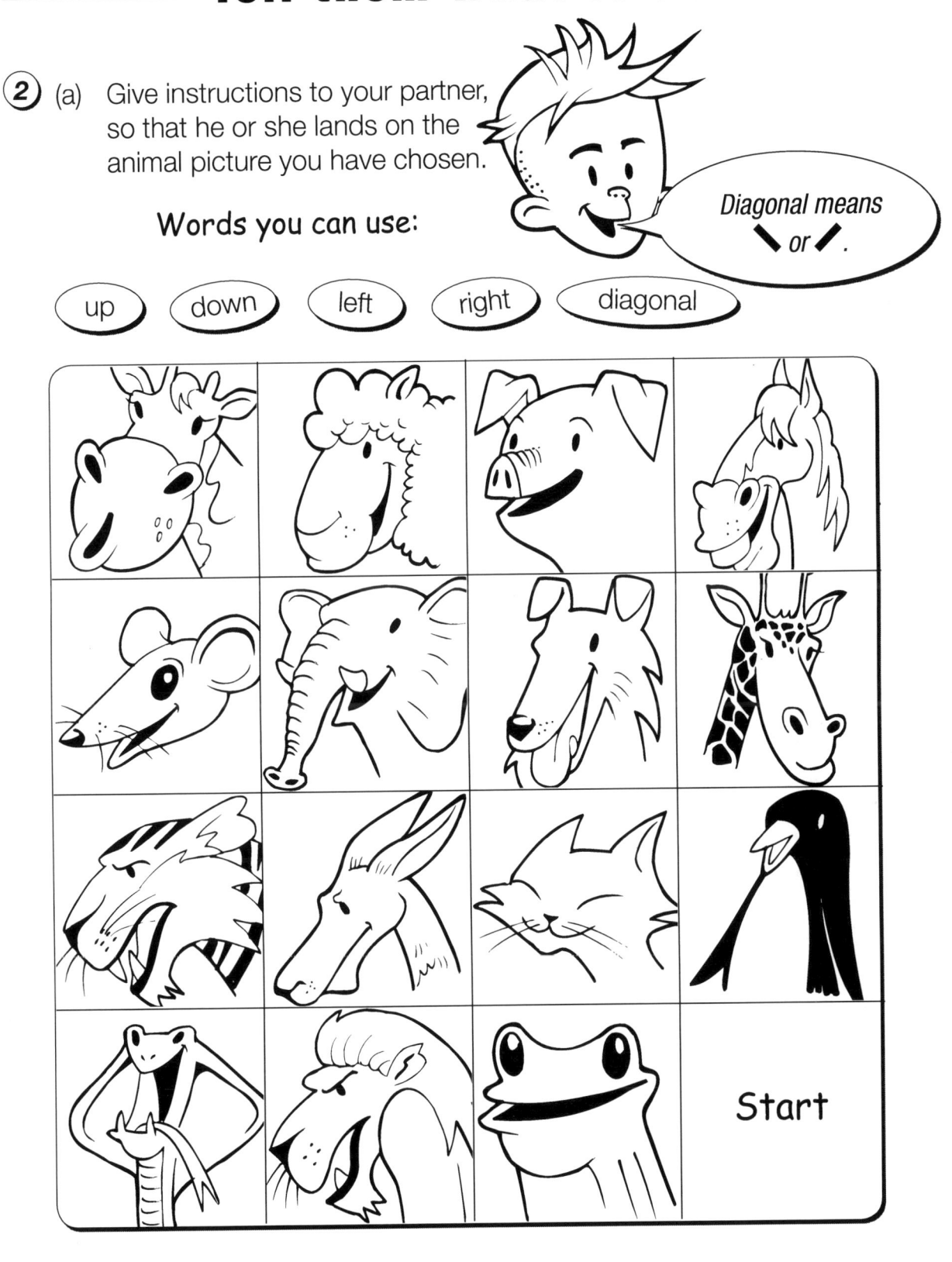

2 (a) Give instructions to your partner, so that he or she lands on the animal picture you have chosen.

Diagonal means \ or /.

Words you can use:

(up) (down) (left) (right) (diagonal)

(b) Did your partner land on the correct animal picture? [yes] [no]

SPEAKING AND LISTENING

NOISY!

TEACHERS NOTES

Objective: Listen to sounds and respond to them.

Activities covered

- Listening to sounds in the school
- Copying the teacher making sounds
- As a class, make sounds as listed on sheet
- **Pair work** – make household noises
- **Pair work** – draw pictures to go with the sounds

Background information

This lesson aims to make children aware of how we can express things through sound, using devices such as onomatopoeia. It also allows them to make sounds – something that they really enjoy!

Before the lesson

Have a list of sounds to make that the children must listen to and copy; for example, ouch, grrrr, psst, bump, sh, plonk, whack, sizzle, crunch, slash, squeak, shatter, snap, rip, tear, crackle, swish, pop, squish, smash, squirt.

The class must be divided into pairs for part of the lesson.

The lesson (Pages 10 and 11)

Children listen to sounds around them.

Children listen to and copy sounds the teacher is making.

Orally, as a class, read through the sound words on the copymaster. Children make the sounds and write down what it reminds them of.

Briefly discuss onomatopoeia. Children can make sounds (one at a time!).

Pair work – Children take turns to make household sounds and their partners must guess what they are; for example, Hoover™, tap, washing machine, lawnmower.

On the copymaster, children draw pictures to go with the given sounds. They can discuss their pictures with their partners.

Children make up and write their own sound word.

Answers

Teacher check

Additional activities

Read poems about sound; for example, *The sound collector* by Roger McGough.

As a class, children can write a sound poem.

Children listen to a CD with animal sounds. Children must guess the animal.

Go outside (preferably in spring or summer) and listen to see how many different types of birds the children can hear.

Stick sound words on objects in the classroom that actually make that sound.

SPEAKING AND LISTENING

TEACHERS NOTES

YOU'RE GIVING IT AWAY!

Objective: Become more adept at using appropriate verbal and non-verbal behaviour in order to secure and maintain the attention of the listener.

Activities covered

- Assessing teacher's mood
- Deciding on people's moods (looking at pictures)
- **Group work** – saying a sentence in a particular mood and guessing other people's moods

Background information

This lesson is about 'reading' tone of voice and body language. These actual terms do not have to be used, as long as children become aware that the way they say something, and the way they hold themselves, may be giving clues as to how they are feeling.

Before the lesson

Have ready statements that can be made to the class, which should be said using different tones of voice and varying forms of body language; for example, Do you think I'm happy with this work? (smiling, clapping hands together), Is this the best class in the school? (hands on hips, angry look, unsmiling), I don't know if I will come to your party (eyes looking down, stooped position, hands behind back, looking unsure), This is an unusual picture (surprised).

Have prepared the manner in which the passage will be read each time.

The class will be divided into groups.

The lesson (Pages 12 and 13)

Discussion: Tell the class that they must listen to your tone of voice and watch your eyes and body language to try to guess how you are feeling. (A little acting is necessary here!) Try to use neutral statements so the children have to read the other signs, as in the examples above.

The teacher reads a passage (see the end of this section), first in a friendly and kind tone, then in an angry and irritable tone.

Children draw faces and write how the teacher sounds for each reading.

Children look at pictures and guess how the people are feeling by reading the body language.

Group work – Children will choose a mood and take turns saying the same sentence, using body language and different tones of voice. The others in the group must guess how they are feeling. Each child can do a few, as well as some other feelings that are not listed.

An example of something that can be read in different tones (although many passages will do!):

'How was my day? Well, those children of mine were quite mad! We did art and there was glitter, paper, glue and paint flying everywhere! The noise level was at danger point! Yes, it's been quite a day!'

Answers

Possible answers:

1. (a) The teacher looks happy/kind/friendly.
   (b) The teacher looks angry/grumpy/mean.
2. (a) The teacher sounds happy.
   (b) The teacher sounds cross.
3. (a) happy/excited/pleased
   (b) shocked/scared/worried
   (c) cross/furious/angry
   (d) upset/frightened/embarrassed
4. Teacher check

Additional activities

The teacher stands and tells the class something, saying it in a monotone, without any expression and using no body language. Then the teacher repeats the information, this time using body language, different tones and expression. Children must point out the difference and say which method is more effective.

Children can give short talks about something familiar to them and use the strategies as discussed in the lesson.

Website on body language: *www.lichaamstaal.com/English* (for teacher).

Read the poem *Waiting for the tone* by Kit Wright or *Said the boy to the dinosaur* by Colin McNaughton. (Read using different tones.)

Children read this poem as a class, using appropriate tones.

The line

I said to the teacher today,
'Anyone can make a mistake!'
'You better mind your manners, Jake!
You're stepping over the line!'

I said to my Mummy today,
'Did no-one teach you how to bake?'
'You better watch what you say, Jake!
You're stepping over the line!'

I said to my Granny today,
'A hundred candles on your cake?'
'You better beware, grandson Jake!
You're stepping over the line!'

I said to my neighbour today,
'Messy lawn! Don't you own a rake?'
'You better be careful, Jake,
You're stepping over the line!'

I said to my sister today,
'That make-up makes you look so fake!'
'You better get out of my sight, Jake!
You're stepping over the line!'

I said to my Daddy today,
'You're so fat that all your bits shake!'
'You better shut up, my son Jake!
You're stepping over the line!'

Where is this line and what does it do?
Can't we move it from time to time?
I'm always stepping over it,
You'd swear I committed a crime!

SPEAKING AND LISTENING

Noisy!

We live in a noisy world!

1) As a class, make these sounds, one by one. Write down what each sound makes you think of.

(a) whoosh

(b) crack

(c) bump

(d) ping

(e) click

(f) whack

(g) creak

(h) buzz

SPEAKING AND LISTENING — Prim-Ed Publishing — www.prim-ed.com

Noisy!

2) Choose a household item and make its noise. Your partner must guess what you are!

3) Draw pictures to go with these sounds.

drip	boom	crash
roar	hiss	bang

4) Make up your own sound word!

Did you know?

Onomatopoeia (what a long word!) is naming a thing or action by the way it sounds.

SPEAKING AND LISTENING

You're giving it away!

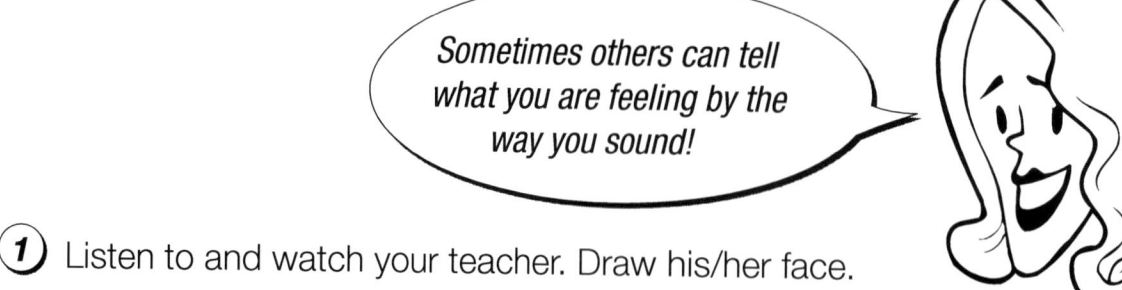

Sometimes others can tell what you are feeling by the way you sound!

1) Listen to and watch your teacher. Draw his/her face.

(a) Reading number 1	(b) Reading number 2

2) How does your teacher sound?

(a) _____

(b) _____

SPEAKING AND LISTENING

You're giving it away!

3 How do you think these people are feeling?

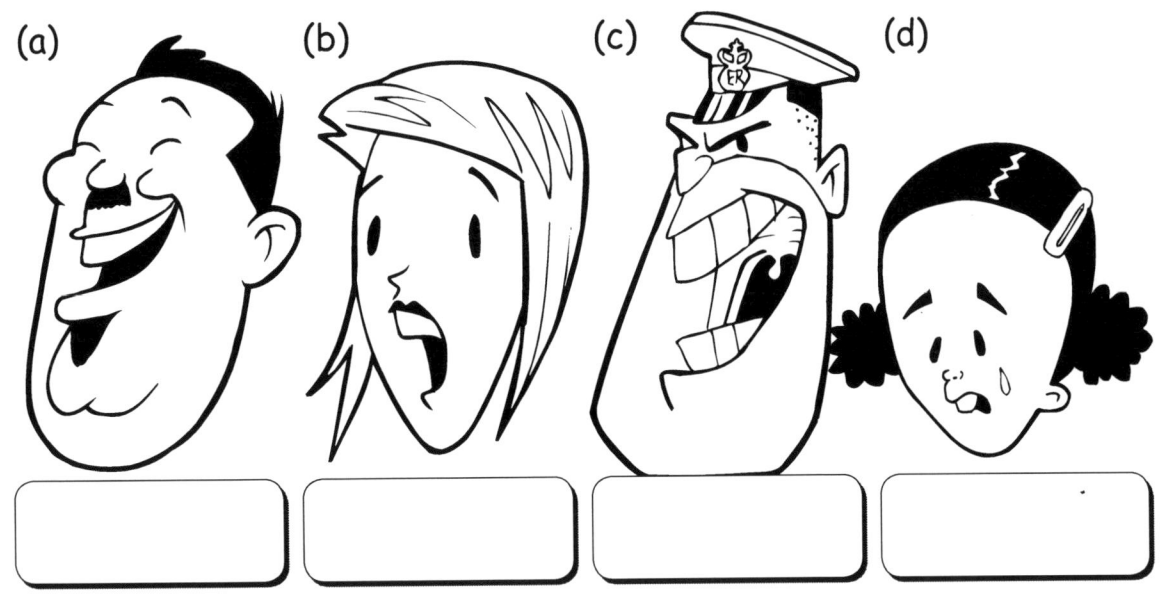

(a) (b) (c) (d)

4 Say the following sentence, choosing one of the moods listed. The others in the group must guess what mood you're in!

I see you have a new puppy.

Moods
happy
excited
bored
worried
angry
tired
grumpy
jealous
proud
afraid
surprised

(a) Write the mood you have chosen.

_____

(b) Did the group guess your mood? yes   no

(c) Choose and write another mood.

_____

(d) Did the group guess your mood? yes   no

SPEAKING AND LISTENING 13

TALKING WITHOUT SPEAKING

TEACHERS NOTES

Objective: Use gesture and movement to extend the meaning of what he/she is saying.

Activities covered

- Watching the teacher and 'reading' the body language
- Filling in speech balloons
- Communicating statements using body language (as a class)
- Playing charades

Background information

This lesson is similar to the previous one but focuses more on how we say things without speaking. Children will be a little more aware now that they are communicating using body language. Do not talk about body language only in this lesson, but also mention it when watching plays, TV programmes, speakers and even each other. The more practice children get in reading the signs, the more adept they will be at it.

Before the lesson

Have body language examples ready that children will 'read'; for example, hands on your head (oh no!), arms in the air (yes!), thumbs up (it's good), wipe your forehead (that's a relief!), hand over your mouth (you're shocked), shaking your head (no), head in your hands (sad, worried).

The lesson (Pages 16 and 17)

The teacher will say different things, as above, without speaking, and children must guess what the teacher is saying.

On the copymaster, children fill in the speech balloons.

As a class, children go through all the statements on the copymaster, giving examples as to how they could communicate them.

Children play charades.

Answers

1. Possible answers include:
   (a) I know the answer!/I've got it!/I will do it.
   (b) You must turn to the right./Please come this way./He's over there.
   (c) I am happy!
   (d) Hello!/Goodbye!
   (e) Please give it to me./I'll take it.
   (f) Come with me./Come here.

2–3. Teacher check

Additional activities

Group work – Children express more complex thoughts to the group; for example, I am tired after a long day./That teacher is really nasty!/I wish it were break now! Statements can be supplied by the teacher, and each child in the group will get a different statement to express. The others need to guess what each child is trying to say.

Website: *www.childdrama.com/mainframe*

(Go to 'Lesson plans', where there are a number of ideas on charades for teachers.)

SPEAKING AND LISTENING

Prim-Ed Publishing   www.prim-ed.com

TEACHERS NOTES

MIME IT!

Objective: Express actions and nursery rhymes using mime.

Activities covered

- Discussing mime
- Watch teacher mime – guess actions
- Children mime situations – rest of class guess
- **Group work** – children mime chosen nursery rhyme, perform it for the class

Background information

Having some experience in body language from previous lessons, children will be able to use these newly acquired skills.

Before the lesson

Have prepared ideas for mime that you can do for the class! Nothing too acrobatic now! Children need to guess what you are doing/feeling; for example, baking a cake, hanging out washing, making breakfast, watching a football match. Try to have a combination of 'acts' showing different feelings and actions.

The class will be divided into groups.

The lesson (Pages 18 and 19)

Discuss what mime is, and how actions are exaggerated to compensate for lack of words.

Mime a few different things for the class. They must guess what you are doing and/or feeling. Some suggestions are listed below.

Children take turns to mime different situations to the class, choosing from the list below or choosing their own. The rest of the class must guess what the child is miming.

Group work – Children mime nursery rhymes.

Ideas for the teacher to mime:

- Tidying your cupboard
- Doing maths homework
- Making a cup of tea
- Building Lego®
- Going shopping
- Washing the dog
- Swatting a fly
- Sitting in an aeroplane
- Gardening
- Being at a fun fair
- Brushing teeth
- Eating breakfast
- Making a bed
- Looking for a key
- Working on a farm
- Painting

Answers

Teacher check

Additional activities

Discuss the different acts that the groups performed and decide as a class how they could be improved.

Children can mime different scenarios from other subjects, such as stories in history.

Look at websites about mime.

www.oao.co.uk/walkabout/mimbo
(This contains pictures of mime artists.)

www.members.tripod.com/~kiko_mime
(This contains video clips of mime.)

SPEAKING AND LISTENING 15

Talking without speaking

Sometimes we say things without talking at all!

1 What do you think these people are saying?

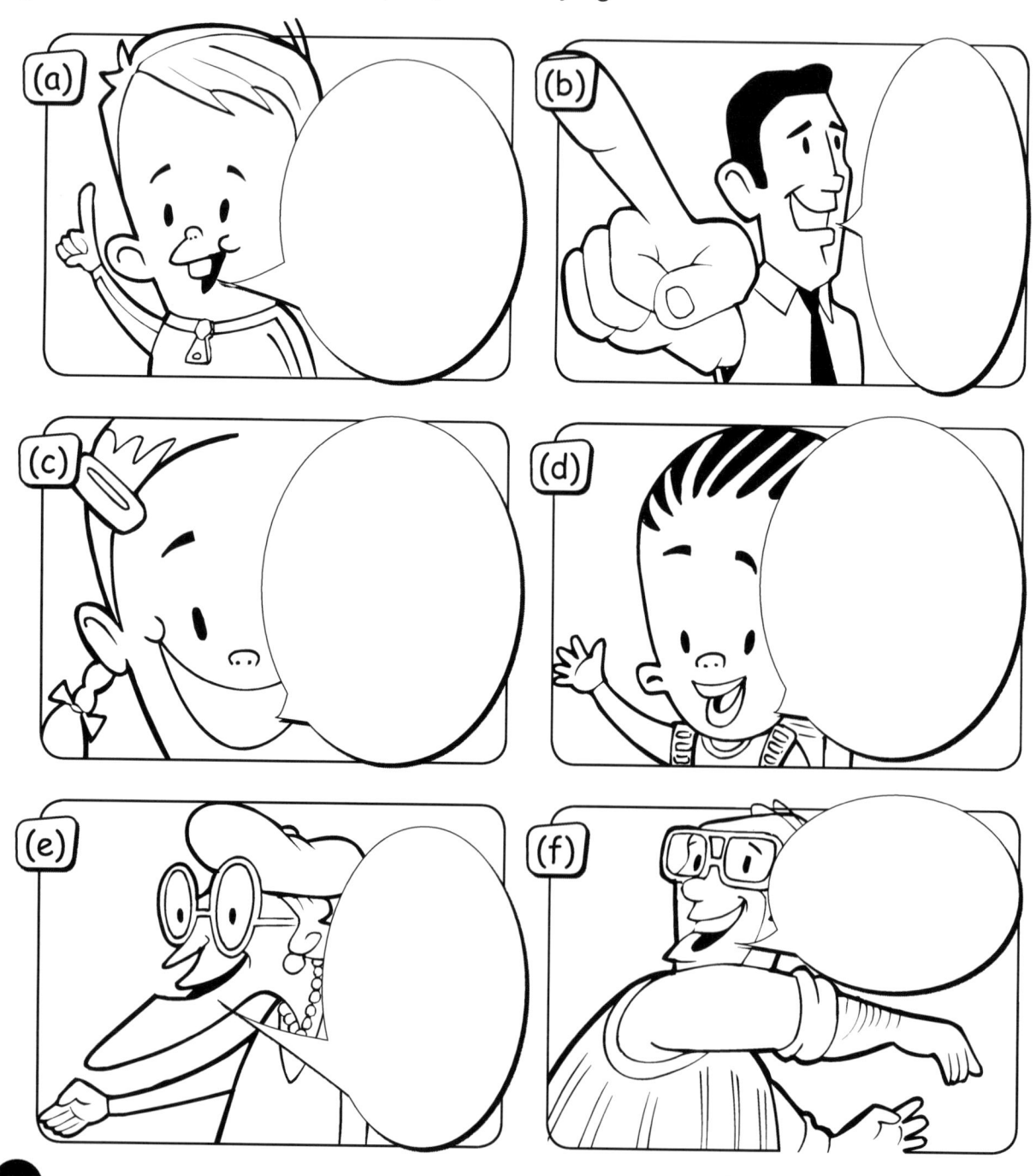

(a)

(b)

(c)

(d)

(e)

(f)

16 SPEAKING AND LISTENING

Prim-Ed Publishing   www.prim-ed.com

Talking without speaking

2 Experiment with saying the following, without using any words. Tick which one was most difficult to do!

(a) It's nice to meet you!

(b) I'm scared!

(c) I'm so excited!

(d) I'm so bored!

(e) You're making too much noise!

(f) I love you!

(g) Go away!

(h) Good day, Your Majesty.

(i) That's excellent!

(j) Please!

(k) I'm shy.

(l) I don't like this!

(m) Definitely not!

If a Frenchman gives you the 'okay' sign, it means 'useless'!

3 Play charades.

SPEAKING AND LISTENING

Mime it!

Mime means to act without words! Your actions alone will have to tell others what you are trying to say!

1) Choose something that you are going to mime for the class. Once you have done your mime, answer these questions:

(a) What did you mime?

(b) Did the class guess correctly?

yes   no

Who guessed your mime?

When you have all done your mime, answer these questions:

(c) Which was the best mime?

(d) Why was it so good?

Mime it!

2 (a) Work as a group. Choose a nursery rhyme that you can mime. Practise it a few times and then present it to the class.

(b) Write down the nursery rhyme you have chosen.

(c) How did your group perform?

Good ☐

Fair ☐

Poor ☐

You use 72 muscles to speak one word!

SPEAKING AND LISTENING 19

READ TOGETHER!

TEACHERS NOTES

Objective: Engage in shared reading activities.

Activities covered

- Reading through a poem as a class
- Answering questions as a class
- Writing a shopping list
- Discussing characters; for example, Old Mother Hubbard and other well-known fictional characters

Background information

Almost any piece of text will do for this lesson, as long as children are reading and sharing it with others.

Before the lesson

Optional – Choose a selection of humorous poems that children could read together. Have ready a list of fictional characters that can be discussed.

The lesson (Pages 22 and 23)

Children can read through the poem on the copymaster, silently first and then as a class.

Remind children that they must speak clearly and read at the same speed as everyone else.

Children answer questions about the poem on the copymaster. Answers can then be discussed with the rest of the class.

Children write a shopping list of essential food items for Mrs Hubbard.

Discuss with the class other fictional characters, such as Cinderella, Bart Simpson, Shrek etc. Discuss not only main characters but others in the story as well.

Answers

Possible answers include:

1. I think Mrs Hubbard was forgetful/kind/silly.
2. Teacher check. (Any age, but not too young, as the poem is about 'old' Mother Hubbard.)
3. She had nothing in her cupboards because she had forgotten to go shopping/there had been heavy snow and she was stuck/someone had burgled her house and taken all the food etc.
4. Shopping list: tea, sugar, bread, cheese, dog food, ham, milk etc. (essential items).

Additional activities

Children compare the poem *Poor dog* with the original rhyme, *Old Mother Hubbard*.

Ask children how they would describe their own character.

Recommended reading: *You're not going out like that!* by Paul Cookson, books by Dr Seuss, *Colin* by Allen Ahlberg, *Dave Dirt's Christmas presents* by Kit Wright, *I'm much better than you!* by Colin McNaughton and *Telling teacher* by Gervase Phinn.

Children makes up their own *Old Mother Hubbard* rhyme – display these.

In groups, children can amend and improve the given poem.

Read children the following poem and discuss when they have felt the same way.

Not yet

We've travelled so long,
We're close now I bet,
It seems so familiar,
Are we there yet?

I've sat here so long,
I am wet with sweat,
My trousers are soggy,
Are we there yet?

The scenery is boring.
Don't say, "Soon, pet!"
I've seen too many trees,
Are we there yet?

This car is so crowded,
We should've taken a jet,
My legs will have blood clots,
Are we there yet?

If I shut up now
Then what will I get?
I'll twiddle my thumbs, but
Are we there yet?

I can't take much more,
I'm starting to fret,
Oh, we've arrived?
Can we go home yet?

SPEAKING AND LISTENING

| TEACHERS NOTES | | **MAKE IT RIGHT!** |

Objective: Self-correct reading errors when what he/she reads does not make sense.

Activities covered

- **Pair work** – reading and correcting a passage
- Trying to figure out pronunciation of harder words
- **Pair work** – reading a poem without any mistakes

Background information

Fluency in reading is something that improves with practice, so children should be given the opportunity to read aloud in class. Encourage understanding and support for children who have reading weaknesses so those who do struggle to read aloud are never ridiculed. Children must at all times be encouraged to self-correct their errors when reading. Tell children they must listen to what they read so that if it does not make sense they know they have made a mistake. If a mistake has been made, it is better for the child to read the sentence again to try to find the mistake himself or herself. (But this should not be a humiliating experience.) This is a longer process but will get children to listen to themselves. If mistakes are still not spotted, then the teacher or fellow children should help.

Before the lesson

The class needs to be divided into pairs.

The lesson (Pages 24 and 25)

Explain to the children that there are no spelling errors in the paragraph, but there are other mistakes.

In pairs, children read through the given paragraph and correct it as they go along. Incorrect words can be crossed out and the correct word written above.

Pairs must then read aloud the new paragraph.

Still in pairs, children attempt to read harder words and give themselves a score out of 10.

This would be a good time to discuss reading aloud in class and how children read at different paces etc. Pose the question: What should we do if someone in the class is struggling to read a word? Stress to children that they must never make fun of anyone's reading.

Still in pairs, children read the poem *Thank goodness* to each other, making as few mistakes as possible. The children may choose to read the poem quietly to themselves a few times before reading it to their partner. The teacher may need to assist with the pronunciation of monkey breeds.

Answers

1. The passage should read:
   Do you **like** doughnuts?
   Doughnuts **were** invented by a fussy **schoolboy**! He told **his** mum that the buns she **made** were soggy **in** the middle. The boy said she should **cut** a hole in them. She did, and her new ring **cakes** were delicious. Not long after, she **began** to sell them!

2–4. Teacher check.

Additional activities

Read a class reader and always give all children the opportunity to read aloud.

Have lists of harder words to read and also discuss their meanings.

Slowly read the passage below about Dr Seuss to the children. Can they spot the mistakes?

All about Dr Seuss

Dr Seuss has written and illustrated many children's book, most of them funny. He was born on 1904 on the USA. Her parents were German so he spoke both English and German at homes. He start drawing when he was just five year old. Later in his life, Dr Seuss and his wife start a company to make books that were easy for read. His most popular books are *Green eggs and ham* and *The cat in the hat*. He became very famous because peoples like the way the words rhymed and also the very funny picture. He died in 1991, at the age of 87.

Have you read any of his books?

SPEAKING AND LISTENING

Read together!

Reading together as a class is harder than you think! Make sure that your voice is clear and that you keep the same pace as the rest of the class.

Read this poem aloud and together, as a class:

Poor dog!

Old Mother Hubbard went to her cupboard,
She was giving Fido dinner.
She hadn't been shopping for ages,
They both seemed to look thinner.

And why was she keeping the bones in the press?
They'd be better off somewhere cool!
And why had she not a morsel of food?
I think Mother Hubbard's a fool!

Did she immediately get in the car that day?
And speed down to the shop?
Did she buy herself some bread and ham,
And Fido a juicy chop?

Mrs Hubbard seems disorganized.
A shopping list needs she,
With rice and tea and vegetables,
And some tins of Pedigree™.

SPEAKING AND LISTENING

Read together!

Answer these questions as a class.

1) What do you think Mrs Hubbard was like?

_____

_____

_____

2) How old do you think she was? ☐

3) Make up a reason as to why she had nothing in her cupboards.

_____

_____

_____

4) Write a shopping list of essential items for her.

Make it right!

Sometimes when we are reading aloud, we make mistakes. When you do make a mistake, try to correct it straight away.

1. Work with a partner. Read this passage to each other, correcting it as you go. Cross out the incorrect words and write the correct words above. There are nine mistakes altogether.

Do you likes doughnuts?

Doughnuts was invented by a fussy schoolboys! He told her mum that the buns she maked were soggy on the middle!

The boy said she should cuts a hole in them. She did, and her new ring cake were delicious. Not long after, she begins to sell them!

2. Read the passage without any mistakes.

Never be in a rush when you read!

Make it right!

3 (a) Try to read these words.

congratulations	scientific
phenomenon	beautifully
illustration	probably
delightful	understand
hippopotamus	flabbergasted

Warning! Some words may be difficult!

(b) How many could you read out of 10? ☐

4 Work in pairs. Try to read this poem without making any mistakes.

Thank goodness!

I **am** glad I am not a monkey,
A marmoset or a baboon,
I'd have to eat insects for breakfast,
And dine on bananas at noon.

I **am** glad I am not a monkey,
A mangabey or capuchin,
I'd have to hang onto my mother,
And scrounge for snacks in the bin!

I **am** glad I am not a monkey,
A macaque or a chimpanzee,
I'd have to hang upside down by my tail,
And spend my life in a tree!

I **am** glad I am not a monkey,
Or a tamarin all in a flap,
I'd have to nibble my sister's fleas,
I am glad I am a chap!

PAST AND FUTURE

TEACHERS NOTES

Objective: Talk about and reflect on past and present experiences and plan, predict, anticipate and speculate about future and imaginary experiences.

Activities covered

- Answering questions about the past
- Drawing and labelling a picture of a future classroom
- Discussing all answers within their groups

Background information

This lesson gives children the opportunity to think about past events and to think about what the future may hold. It is a good lesson for class discussion and imagination! It might also be a time to mention the words 'past', 'present' and 'future'.

Before the lesson

The class is divided into groups after the copymasters have been completed.

The lesson (Pages 28 and 29)

Children draw a picture of their earliest memory and write a sentence about it.

Children write about a good and bad thing that has happened to them.

Discuss with the children modern inventions and what might be invented in the future.

Children think about how a classroom may look in 100 years time. Children draw and label the classroom.

Group work – Children discuss their answers and futuristic classroom design with their group.

Answers

1–3. Teacher check
4. Possible futuristic classrooms? Robots teaching the class (that would be great!), fridges in the classroom, lessons being taught by a computer, space age furniture, super comfy, adjustable school chairs, whiteboards that clean themselves, remote controlled blinds and windows, self-cleaning system, coffee, tea and soup machines, game arcades for break time; the list is endless!
5. Teacher check

Additional activities

Children bring photos to school of when they were younger and tell the class about the photo.

Children discuss what occupations they would like to have.

Children discuss what a house might look like in 100 years time.

Children make time lines of their lives.

Children read and discuss modern-day inventions.

The teacher can present information on what life was like 100 years ago, and children can make simple comparisons with life today.

Read these poems with the class: *My pet mouse* by David Whitehead and *Inventions I'd like to see* by Douglas Florian.

Look at websites to do with modern gadgets and gizmos; for example, the futuristic house, all controlled via the Internet, where one can switch the TV on/off, open the blinds, switch on the electric blanket, lock and unlock doors, all from anywhere in the world.

The children can have a display in the classroom of old and modern objects that they bring from home.

Children can read poetry about school days in the past and compare them with school today.

SPEAKING AND LISTENING

TEACHERS NOTES

IT'S NOT NICE!

> *Objective: Experiment with more elaborate vocabulary and sentence structure to extend and explore meaning.*

Activities covered

- **As a class** – replacing words
- **As a class** – writing words which describe nouns
- **As a class** – filling in words (describing words) to complete the story

Background information

This lesson aims to show children how to make their writing more interesting and varied. The lesson focuses on adjectives, and it should be pointed out how the meaning of the sentence is extended, with each describing word giving more information. Using more descriptive words in oral language obviously means more interesting conversation and this should be explained to the children.

Before the lesson

Have ready examples of how adding describing words enhances our writing and speaking.

The lesson (Pages 30 and 31)

Discuss with the children how adding more details to a sentence gives more information and makes the sentence more interesting. Give many examples: The dog was nice – The fluffy, white dog was friendly. (Which sentence paints a clearer picture?) The man drove the car – The rich man drove the flashy, silver car. The boy ate a pizza – The hungry boy ate a huge, anchovy pizza.

Children make the sentences more interesting by replacing the adjective 'nice' with more interesting adjectives that might give more information. These sentences can be discussed as a class. Mention the word 'adjective', although this will not have to be learnt.

As a class – Children think of describing words to describe the nouns given. Children need to write only one.

As a class – Children fill in the blanks with describing words to complete the story.

Individually, children can try to improve on the words in the passage.

Answers

Answers will vary, but could include:
1. (a) The **brave** dog chased the **nasty** man.
   (b) The **angry** teacher gave me a **boring** book.
   (c) The **enormous** monster ate my **delicious** dinner.
2. shop – cramped, child – bold, sweet – sticky, shoe – smelly, book – thick, night – gloomy, teacher – lovely, cat – scrawny etc.
3. nervous, silent, single, funny, green, hard, hot, webbed, sharp, terrified, monstrous
4. Teacher check

Additional activities

In pairs, children must have a conversation using as many descriptive words as possible.

Repeat the same type of lesson using adverbs, synonyms, conjunctions etc. to make children's writing better and, consequently, make them aware that it will also make their conversation more interesting!

Children can display describing words in the classroom to do with school or another topic being covered in another subject.

Read descriptive poetry; for example, *The ghost teacher* by Allen Ahlberg.

Read this poem with the class; children must try to identify the describing words:

Ally

There's a person who loves me,
no matter what I do.
She always thinks I'm special,
talented and true.

She thinks I'm the handsomest
in the whole entire school.
Anyone who's not my friend
must surely be a fool.

She thinks I'm a genius,
who will one day rule this earth.
She says I've shown potential
ever since my birth.

She states there isn't a better child,
if you looked from east to west.
She makes me feel so warm and safe,
my grandma is the best.

SPEAKING AND LISTENING 27

Past and future

1) What is the earliest thing you can remember?

How far back can you remember?

(a) Draw it.

(b) Write a sentence about it.

_____

_____

_____

2) Write about something good that has happened to you.

_____

_____

_____

SPEAKING AND LISTENING

Past and future

3) Write about something bad that has happened to you.

_____

_____

_____

4) What do you think a classroom will look like in 100 years time? Draw it and label the different parts.

> *Did you know?*
> *Some scientists believe that human beings of the future will have fewer teeth, no hair and no little toes!*

5) Discuss all your answers with your group.

SPEAKING AND LISTENING 29

It's not nice!

Using describing words can make our conversation and writing more interesting!

1) Replace the adjective 'nice' with more interesting adjectives.

(a) The **nice** dog chased the **nice** man.

The _____ dog chased the _____ man.

(b) The **nice** teacher gave me a **nice** book.

The _____ teacher gave me a _____ book.

(c) The **nice** monster ate my **nice** dinner.

The _____ monster ate my _____ dinner.

2) What words could you use to describe these?

shop		child	
sweet		shoe	
book		night	
teacher (be nice!)		cat	

SPEAKING AND LISTENING — 30 — Prim-Ed Publishing — www.prim-ed.com

It's not nice!

Describing words are called adjectives.

3 (a) Add describing words to this passage and then read it out loud to the class.

The _____ children sat quietly in the _____ classroom. Nobody made a _____ sound. Their _____ teacher had always seemed a little strange, but not this strange! Her skin had turned _____ and _____ scales started to grow. She started blowing _____ flames from her mouth. _____ wings started to sprout out of her sides and her fingernails became _____ claws. The _____ class watched in horror as their teacher turned into a _____ dragon.

(b) Has this ever happened to your class? [yes] [no]

4 Can you make your words even more interesting? Give it a try!

ORDER!

TEACHERS NOTES

Objective: Experiment with word order and examine its implications for meaning and clarity.

Activities covered

- **Pair work** – answering 'yes' or 'no' (does changing word order change the meaning?)
- **Pair work** – changing word order in the sentences
- **Class work** – reading aloud and changing word order to create a new menu

Background information

The children must experiment with word order in this lesson – does changing the word order in a sentence change the meaning? Sometimes the meaning changes and sometimes it doesn't. Once children have had practice in this, they will be ready to move on and actually improve sentences by changing the word order.

Before the lesson

The class will be divided into pairs at the start of the lesson.

Have ready examples of sentences where the word order can be changed orally as a class.

The lesson (Pages 34 and 35)

As a class, read sentences given by the teacher. (Sentences can be written on the board.)

Children decide whether changing the word order changes the meaning of the sentence. Examples of sentences that can be used: The angry dog chased the scared cat – The angry cat chased the scared dog./The wobbly jelly was eaten by the big man. – The big man was eaten by the wobbly jelly.

Children divide into pairs.

Children answer 'yes' or 'no' as to whether changing the word order changes the meaning of the sentence.

Children change the meaning of the sentences by changing the words around.

Children read the menu as a class. The children change the words around in a menu to make a completely new (but awful!) one; for example, cereal with carrots, strawberry sandwich, toast with peas, orange potatoes. Early finishers could draw one of the new meals on the back of their copymaster.

Answers

1. (a) No (b) Yes (c) No (d) Yes
2. Answers will vary, but could include:
   (a) My spooky brother screamed when he saw the little ghost.
   (b) A hungry apple ate my juicy sister.
   (c) The class shouted at the naughty teacher.
3–4. Teacher check

Additional activities

Children read through a poem and change the word order; for example, *I would sooner* by Gervase Phinn.

Children improve sentences by changing the word order in awkward sounding sentences; for example, The chair was sat on by the cat. – The cat sat on the chair.

SPEAKING AND LISTENING

TEACHERS NOTES

WHAT DID WE TALK ABOUT?

Objective: Focus on the subject matter under discussion, sustain a conversation on it and answer questions about the conversation.

Activities covered

- Discussing pets as a class
- Answering questions concerning discussion

Background information

The teacher can initiate conversation by introducing the subject – the children must keep the discussion going and stick to the topic at hand! Any subject can be discussed here, but 'pets' has been chosen, as most children either have pets or would like to have them! The discussion must only be about pets, and not other animals.

Keep control by insisting that children put up their hands to have their say, and that others must listen to what they are saying.

Encourage quieter children to talk too, by asking a question or two if they do not volunteer information themselves.

Before the lesson

Have information ready about pets to discuss with the class.

Collect some pictures of pets and unusual pets, like special breeds of cats or dogs.

The lesson (Pages 36 and 37)

Present your own information to the class about pets, covering the following points:

- Different types of pets: cats/dogs/horses/rabbits/birds/hamsters/fish etc.
- More unusual types of pets: snakes/monkeys/wild animals etc.
- How to take care of your pet: Feed it every day./Always provide fresh water for it to drink./Keep its cage/tank/kennel etc. clean./Give it shelter in bad weather./Take it to the vet if it is sick./Keep it safe; for example, have fences for a dog./Give it plenty of love!/Brush the animal's coat (if it has one!).

Hold a class discussion on pets, with children taking turns to speak or ask questions. If someone starts talking about something else, guide him or her back to the topic.

Children answer questions in their copymaster and draw their own pet.

Answers

1. pets
2–3. Teacher check
4. (a), (d) and (e)
5. Teacher check

Additional information

Complete the same lesson with different topics, perhaps a topic from another subject.

Group work – Each child gets a card with a topic of conversation – he or she must initiate conversation and the whole group must keep it going.

Website: for taking care of animals, look at
www.hsus.org/pets/pet_care

Have a display in the classroom of the children's pets – with photos or pictures they have drawn.

Children read poems as a class about pets; for example, *The lion's den* by Colin McNaughton, *Strangeways* by Roger McGough, and *Our cat cuddles* by Gervase Phinn.

SPEAKING AND LISTENING

Order!

Changing the order of the words in a sentence can sometimes change the meaning!

1. Read these sentences aloud. Does changing the word order change the meaning?

(a) My fluffy, black cat jumped onto the gate.
Onto the gate my fluffy, black cat jumped.   yes / no

(b) My big brother has a wild bird.
My wild brother has a big bird.   yes / no

(c) I had a bowl of cereal this morning.
This morning I had a bowl of cereal.   yes / no

(d) I slept in my bed after school.
After bed, I slept in my school.   yes / no

2. Change the order of the words in these sentences so that they **do not** mean the same thing.

(a) My little brother screamed when he saw the spooky ghost.

_____

(b) My hungry sister ate a juicy apple.

_____

(c) The teacher shouted at the naughty class.

_____

Order!

3) Read this menu.

Breakfast

Cereal with milk
Fresh fruit
Strawberry yoghurt
Toast with cheese
Orange juice

Lunch

Ham and salad sandwich
Vegetable soup

Dinner

Chicken with peas, carrots, potatoes and rice
Apple and nut pie with cream

4) Change the words around in this menu to make a completely new one!

Breakfast

_____
_____
_____
_____
_____
_____

Lunch

_____
_____
_____

Dinner

_____
_____
_____

SPEAKING AND LISTENING

What did we talk about?

1 What did the class discuss?

_____

_____

2 Name four pets children in your class own.

(a) _____

(b) _____

(c) _____

(d) _____

Always take good care of your pets!

3 Write three ways to take care of pets.

(a) _____

_____

_____

(b) _____

_____

_____

(c) _____

_____

_____

36 SPEAKING AND LISTENING   Prim-Ed Publishing   www.prim-ed.com

What did we talk about?

4) Tick the sentences that match the talk we had today.

(a) Hamsters need to have their cages cleaned. ☐

(b) Lions and leopards are part of the cat family. ☐

(c) Sharks can have several rows of teeth. ☐

(d) Our pets need to be fed every day. ☐

(e) Some people keep monkeys as pets. ☐

(f) Cows and sheep are farm animals. ☐

5) (a) Write a sentence about your pet or a friend's pet.

_____

_____

_____

(b) Draw the pet.

SUMMER FUN!

TEACHERS NOTES

Objective: Initiate discussions, respond to the initiatives of others and have practice in taking turns.

Activities covered

- Discussing summer activities as a class
- Discussing the most popular activities
- Answering questions about their summer
- Writing an acrostic poem about summer

Background information

Children usually enjoy speaking about their experiences but are often reluctant to allow others to have their say. This is especially true when they are speaking about something they are interested in! The teacher must point out that each child will be given a chance to speak and no one is to speak while others are talking. A time limit could be set for each child.

Before the lesson

Prepare cards with numbers on for the class. Children will pull these numbers from a 'hat' and this will give them the order in which they are speaking.

The lesson (Pages 40 and 41)

On the copymaster, children write a list of activities they do in the summer.

Children pick a number from a hat.

Each child gets a chance to speak about their summer.

The teacher writes headings on the board as the activity is mentioned. If the activity is already mentioned, the teacher places a tick under that heading. Examples of headings might be: football, cinema, holidays, friends, chores, shopping, swimming.

Once everyone has spoken, the class must look at the board and discuss the findings. What activities are the most popular?

Children complete the questions on their copymaster.

Children write an acrostic poem, using each letter of the word 'summer'.

Answers

Answers will vary.

Additional activities

Group work – Children look at different paintings depicting summer and each child gives his/her comments, and why he/she likes it or doesn't like it.

Website: (dangers of sunburn)
www.bbc.co.uk/science/hottopics/sunshine/dangers.shtml

The class can have a 'summer' display in the classroom. Include in the display the word 'summer' with all the words that the children had for each letter.

Discuss with the class: What is a typical British summer?

The class can read poems about summer; for example, *Things to do on the first day of the summer holidays* by Fred Sedgwick.

The class can read and discuss the following:

Pack your bags

Carrying a map, but getting lost,
Buying things, not knowing the cost,
Bearing luggage that weighs a ton,
Turning red from the raging sun.

Eating food that makes you ill,
Reeling from the restaurant bill,
Being patient with a flight delay,
Walking airports the entire day.

Listening to language you've never heard,
Not comprehending a single word,
Looking for statues and ageless sights,
Aching from walking and sleepless nights.

Protecting yourself from foreign bugs,
Looking for toilets, avoiding thugs,
Yes, travelling is hard, and it is dear,
But we'll do it again, same time next year.

SPEAKING AND LISTENING

Prim-Ed Publishing   www.prim-ed.com

TEACHERS NOTES

HOW DO YOU DO?

Objective: Engage in real and imaginary situations to perform different social functions.

Activities covered

- Discussing being polite and having good manners
- Filling in speech balloons, responding to statements with written dialogue
- Discussing answers as a class – some children demonstrating
- **Pair work** – role-playing different social functions and assessing them

Background information

Social functions have to be demonstrated and practised. This lesson allows children to role-play different social functions.

Before the lesson

The class will be divided into pairs.

Examples of different social functions need to be explained to the class.

The lesson (Pages 42 and 43)

Discuss with the class politeness when speaking to people and the importance of it. Get children to give examples of what being polite means.

Discuss: How should we greet someone? How could we apologise if we've done something wrong? How could we say thank you if someone compliments us? How could we ask for help? How do we compliment others?

Children fill in speech balloons on their copymaster.

Children respond to statements by writing something they would say.

As a class, discuss the answers the children have written. Some children could demonstrate the way it should be done.

Pair work – Children role-play three social functions and assess how good they were at each.

Answers

Answers will vary, but could include:
1. (a) 'I am fine thank you.'/'Fine, thanks, and you?'
   (b) 'I am sorry. Can I do it now?'
   (c) 'Thank you very much for this lovely gift.'
2. (a) 'Thanks, Mum, for the delicious dinner.'
   (b) 'Excuse me, could you help me please?'
   (c) 'I apologise for doing that. It won't happen again.'
3–4. Teacher check

Additional activities

Practise other social functions; for example, explaining to someone that you are lost (mention about talking to strangers), telling the waiter what you would like to order.

Role-play different telephone conversations; for example, making dinner reservations, having a 'chat', requesting information, making a complaint.

Role-play an important/famous visitor coming to the school.

Discuss different social functions in different cultures.

SPEAKING AND LISTENING

Summer fun!

Summer usually means no school for a while!

1 Things I do in the summer:

(a) _____

(b) _____

(c) _____

(d) _____

2 What are the most popular things that children in your class do in the summer?

Listen to others when they are speaking!

(a) _____

(b) _____

(c) _____

(d) _____

3 Draw a picture of your summer.

SPEAKING AND LISTENING

Summer fun!

4 What things could you do if you got bored during the summer?

(a) _____

_____

(b) _____

_____

(c) _____

_____

(d) _____

_____

5 Describe summer holidays by using each letter of 'summer'.

S _____
U _____
M _____
M _____
E _____
R _____

Did you know? The sun is one of the stars of the Milky Way.

How do you do?

Whoever you are speaking to, it is important that you are polite! Use the words 'please' and 'thank you' whenever you can!

1) Write your replies in the speech balloons.

(a) Hello, how are you?

(b) You did not finish your work!

(c) Here is a small gift for your birthday.

SPEAKING AND LISTENING

How do you do?

In Japan, you should bow when greeting.

2 What would you say in these situations?

(a) The dinner was delicious and you want Mum to know you appreciated it.

_____

_____

(b) You are looking for something in the shop.

_____

_____

(c) You were nasty to your good friend.

_____

_____

3 Work with a partner. Role-play these scenes.

(a) Thank a friend for helping you out. /5

(b) Apologise to a family member for something that you did. /5

(c) Ask the teacher for help with something you don't understand. /5

4 How did you do? Give yourself a mark out of 5 for each!

YOUR PROJECT

TEACHERS NOTES

Objective: Find information and share it with others.

Activities covered

- Researching a topic
- Completing the copymaster, writing keywords and drawing a picture
- Presenting a talk
- Self-assessment

Background information

This lesson focuses on research; the oral part is the presentation of information to the class.

Before the lesson

Children can either be given a topic or choose one themselves. Make sure there are sufficient resources available in the school for the children to gather their information. It is advisable for children to have different topics; otherwise, unless you have a very large library, children will need to share books and this will slow down the process! Perhaps the teacher could see what information is available and allocate topics accordingly.

Children must be given time to complete their research.

Have ready examples showing what keywords are.

The lesson (Pages 46 and 47)

Tell the class what it is you expect of them; for example, how long the project should be, how long the talk should be, what their picture could be of.

Explain to children what keywords are and give examples; for example, the weather today is very stormy and dark – I think it's going to rain in a minute. Keywords: weather – stormy, dark, rain.

Talk through the example about 'dogs' on the copymaster.

Children complete their research and write keywords on their copymaster.

Children draw a picture relating to their topic. They should show this picture as part of their talk.

Children present their talk to the class.

Children rate their talk: good/average/poor.

Children discuss ways in which their talk could be improved.

Answers

Teacher check

Additional activities

Children must bring an article/advert from a newspaper or magazine and tell the class about it.

Children can search for information on the Internet which ties in with another subject; for example, flowers in science, mountains in geography. Internet usage must, of course, always be supervised.

SPEAKING AND LISTENING

Prim-Ed Publishing   www.prim-ed.com

TEACHERS NOTES

CHILDREN'S MEALS

Objective: Experience an abundance or oral language activity when preparing a writing task.

Activities covered

- Discussing topic as a class (discussing at length!)
- **Pair work** – planning and designing a poster for a restaurant
- Displaying work
- Discussing each other's projects

Background information

Oral language often precedes writing activities.

The idea of this lesson is to generate many ideas and thoughts before the writing process begins.

Discussion should inspire the children to write. Spellings and ideas on the board can facilitate the writing process.

Before the lesson

Have ideas ready for class discussion.

After the discussion, the class will be divided into pairs.

The lesson (Pages 48 and 49)

Have a discussion on restaurants; for example, food served there, how a 'children only' restaurant might be, menu for children only, possible special areas in restaurants for children, prices, waiters and waiters' uniforms, possible activities there could be to keep the children happy, decor.

The teacher writes ideas on the board.

Talk about an advertising poster. Tell children to pretend that they are opening a children's restaurant in their local area. In pairs, children must make up an advert for the restaurant, which should include: name of restaurant, address, telephone no., type of food, opening times, attractions etc. (A list can be written on the board.)

Pair work – Children design a poster on their copymaster for their restaurant, in rough. Children draw their posters neatly, doing their best work.

Children give their restaurant a star rating.

Adverts can be displayed for the rest of the class to see. Briefly discuss the different adverts the children have made, what works and why it works.

Answers

Teacher check

Additional activities

Children make a TV advertisement for their restaurant.

Children design a 'children only' menu.

Read aloud and discuss a book/poem; for example, *The rascally cake* by Jeanne Willis and Korky Paul. Children read aloud as a class, and then in groups, and come up with their own recipe to create a monster, which they then read to the class.

Discuss with the class local places to eat. What are the children's favourites and why?

The teacher can check to see if there are websites for local restaurants, and allow the children to look at them.

Read to the class poems about food; for example, *Nothing tastes quite like a gerbil* by Tony Langham and *The cake that makes you scream* by Dave Ward.

SPEAKING AND LISTENING

Your project

1) A child has completed a project about dogs. Read the notes he/she wrote to help with a talk.

It is project time! You will give a talk on your project.

Dogs
1st part of talk: food
    Keywords: tins of dog food, bones, water
2nd part of talk: exercise
    Keywords: walks, toys, fetching sticks
3rd part of talk: care
    Keywords: bath, grooming, vets

2) What topic have you chosen? _____

3) Write down notes, using keywords, to help you remember what you are going to say.

1st part of talk: _____
    Keywords: _____

2nd part of talk: _____
    Keywords: _____

3rd part of talk: _____
    Keywords: _____

Your project

4) Draw a picture of your topic and write one sentence about it.

5) Read through your keywords a few times before you stand up and give your talk. Good luck!

6) Tick how well you thought you spoke.

well ☐   quite well ☐   not so well ☐

7) What was the best part of your talk?

8) How could you make your talk better?

Children's meals

1 (a) What is your favourite restaurant? _____

(b) What is your favourite meal? _____

(c) What would you like to see on a restaurant menu? _____
_____

(d) What would you charge for this? (e) Should there be an area in restaurants for children only?

£ _____

[yes] [no]

2 What activities could you have in a restaurant to keep children happy?
_____
_____
_____

Everyone loves eating out!

3 You are going to design a poster for a children only restaurant. Plan what you will include in your poster below.

Name of restaurant: _____

Address: _____
_____

Telephone number: _____

Opening times: _____

Type of food: _____
_____

Other attractions: _____

Children's meals

4) Use your ideas to create a poster for a children only restaurant. Plan your poster, in rough, below.

5) What is the best part of your poster?

_____

_____

6) How could you improve your poster?

_____

_____

7) Create a 'best' version of your poster, to display in the classroom.

8) Colour the star rating you would give your restaurant (5 stars is the best).

SPEAKING AND LISTENING 49

WRITING FOR YOURSELF

TEACHERS NOTES

Objective: Have regular opportunities to write for himself/herself or for others.

Activities covered

- Writing lists and messages
- Taking notes
- Giving and writing down homework

Background information

The focus of this lesson is slightly different because children are learning to write something that is functional and for themselves. Most writing in school is done for the teacher or for an educational purpose. Children must be made aware of the relevance of writing and that it will be used by them in their everyday lives.

Before the lesson

Have ready examples of times we might write for others or ourselves.

The teacher can hand out scraps of paper, so that the children can write homework that other children are giving them.

The lesson (Pages 52 and 53)

Have a short class discussion on when we might write for others or ourselves outside of school; for example, shopping lists, messages, birthday cards, invitations, notes, letters.

Children write a short Christmas list and birthday message on their copymaster.

As a class, read the speech balloon on the copymaster. As a class, decide what exactly is for homework. Explain to the class that they must read and listen out for just the homework, they needn't write 'keep it neat' etc.

Children write down homework, in note form.

Children stand up in front of the class and give out lots of homework, while other children write down the homework. (I bet they'll be cruel!)

Answers

1–2. Teacher check
3. Homework:
   maths: p. 13, questions 4 and 5
   English: story, 5 spellings, read
   Geography: colour map
4. Teacher check

Additional activities

Any of the examples already mentioned can be written; for example, writing a telephone message, writing a party invitation, writing a card or postcard, making a shopping list, filling in simple forms.

Children write a letter to a relative or friend who lives far away and the teacher must post the letters.

The class can read the following poem:

Anything but this

I'd rather be skiing on mountain slopes,
than working at this table.
I'd rather be climbing the Eiffel Tower,
or chasing after sable.

I'd rather be swimming in an aqua sea,
than sitting here doing these sums.
I'd rather be skateboarding in LA
where winter never comes.

I'd rather be walking in the Amazon Jungle,
than reading through these poems.
I'd rather be meeting ancient tribes
and visiting their homes.

I'd rather be walking China's wall,
than trudging through this work.
I'd rather be diving the Coral Reef,
where sharks and stonefish lurk.

I'd rather be sipping Indian tea,
than learning all these facts,
I'd rather be sitting in the West End,
and watching all the acts.

I'd rather be doing anything else,
I'm sure I know enough.
I'll do my homework later,
or not, and that's just tough.

SPEAKING AND LISTENING

TEACHERS NOTES

DO NOT DISTURB!

Objective: Confer with the teacher and others on the quality of presentation.

Activities covered

- Making a door sign – draft design
- **Group work** – commenting on each other's signs
- Making changes as necessary
- Producing a neat, finished sign

Background information

It is important in this lesson that when children are initially working on their task, they do so quietly without discussing their work with anyone. Children will have the opportunity to take on board comments and suggestions that others make. Stress that children must be honest, but kind, when evaluating each other's work.

This sort of lesson can be done on a frequent basis, especially when work is displayed for others to see. It is important that children learn to make comments that are truthful, but take into account the person's feelings. It is also an opportunity for children to find something positive in other's work. The teacher should step in and do this if everyone is calling someone's work 'weak'.

Children should confer with the teacher on a regular basis. The teacher and children should have a few times a week where they discuss work, preferably on an individual basis (when time allows!).

Before the lesson

The class will be divided into groups.

The lesson (Pages 54 and 55)

Discuss with the class the task they are about to undertake. Explain that they will complete, firstly, a rough draft, of a sign for their bedroom door.

Children must include little clues about themselves in their sign; for example, blue writing if it is their favourite colour, a skateboard if they love skateboarding. They do not have to write 'Do not disturb' but can use 'Jamie's Room' or 'My place' etc.

Children complete a rough draft on their copymaster.

Group work – Each child explains to the group what his/her sign is all about.

The group makes comments about the sign in question, and gives ideas and suggestions on how to make it better.

Children answer Questions 3 and 4 about the comments they received.

Children complete their signs in neat, making any changes necessary.

Children cut out their signs (these could be laminated if the school has a laminator) and hang them on their bedroom door.

Answers

Teacher check

Additional activities

Have a writer's gallery, where good work is displayed. Change this frequently. Teachers can change the focus of 'good work' to include neatest presentation, interesting work, most unusual etc. so that all children get a turn at being in the writer's gallery.

SPEAKING AND LISTENING

Writing for yourself

1 Think of times other than at school when you might have to write. Write a list.

(a) _____

(b) _____

(c) _____

Writing isn't just for school!

2 Two times you might write other than at school are for Christmas and birthdays.

(a) Write a list of things you would like to receive for Christmas. (Don't get too greedy!)

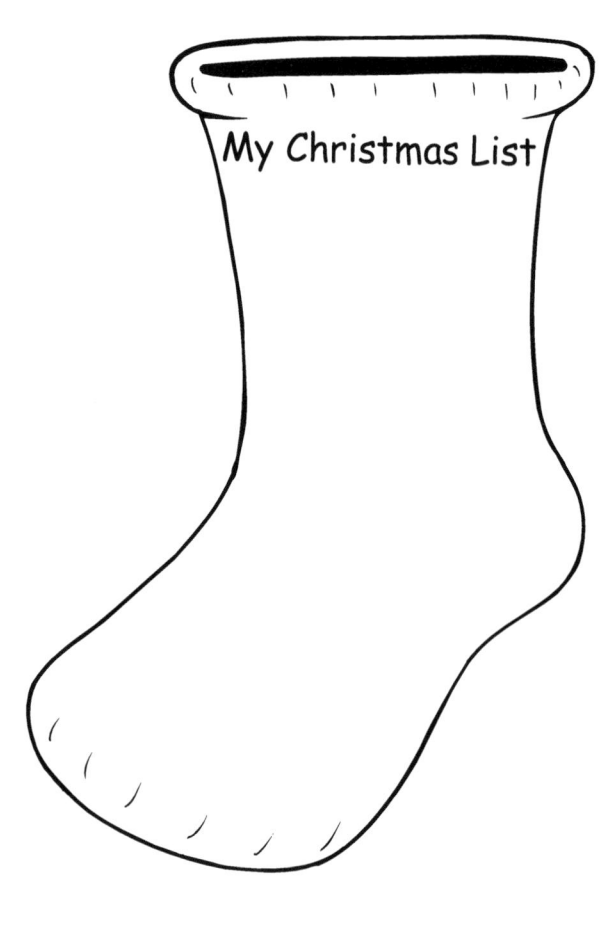

(b) It is your friend's birthday. Write a message to go in his/her birthday card.

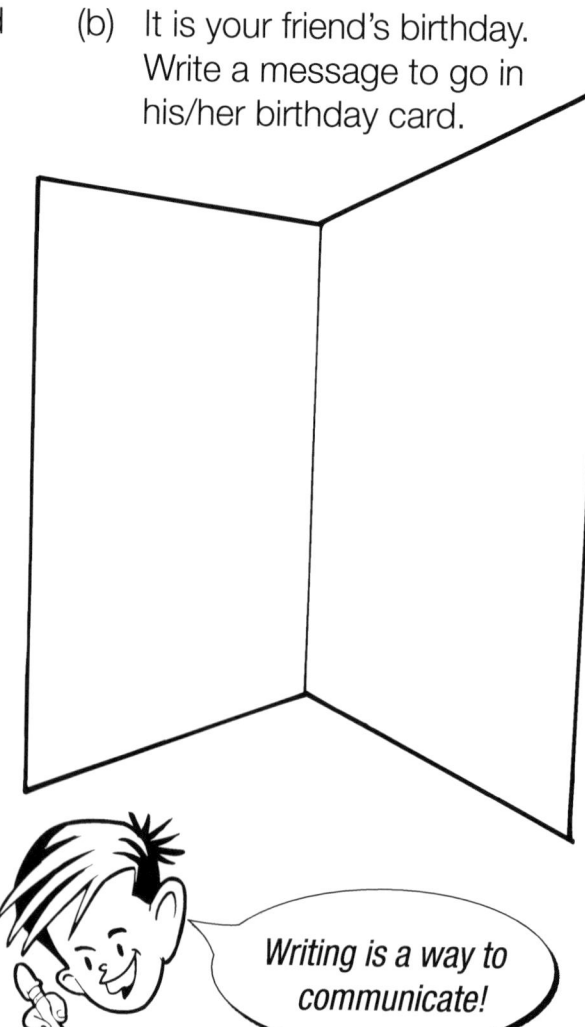

My Christmas List

Writing is a way to communicate!

SPEAKING AND LISTENING

Writing for yourself

3) This teacher is giving a lot of homework! Without repeating his every word, write notes on exactly what is for homework.

> Now, children, you will have quite a bit of homework to do tonight, I'm afraid. It's a rainy day anyway, so at least you'll have something to do! For maths, you must do Questions 4 and 5 on page 13, and keep it neat! For English, you must finish off your story. For geography, you must colour the map. Now, let me see, is that too much? Oh! And of course, you must learn your 5 spellings and do some reading of your own! Is that enough homework? I could give you science, but, no, I'll let you off today.

Homework

_____
_____
_____
_____
_____
_____
_____

4) Stand up in front of the class and give out lots of homework. The class must listen and write it down on a scrap of paper.

How many subjects did you give for homework?

> **Did you know?**
> The earliest writing in Mesopotamia was picture writing, written on clay tablets using long reeds.

SPEAKING AND LISTENING 53

Do not disturb!

You are going to make a bedroom door sign. Then your group is going to say what they think of it! Remember to be honest but kind when talking about someone's work.

1) Design a sign for your bedroom door with your name on it. Include little clues about yourself in your sign. Complete your rough draft here.

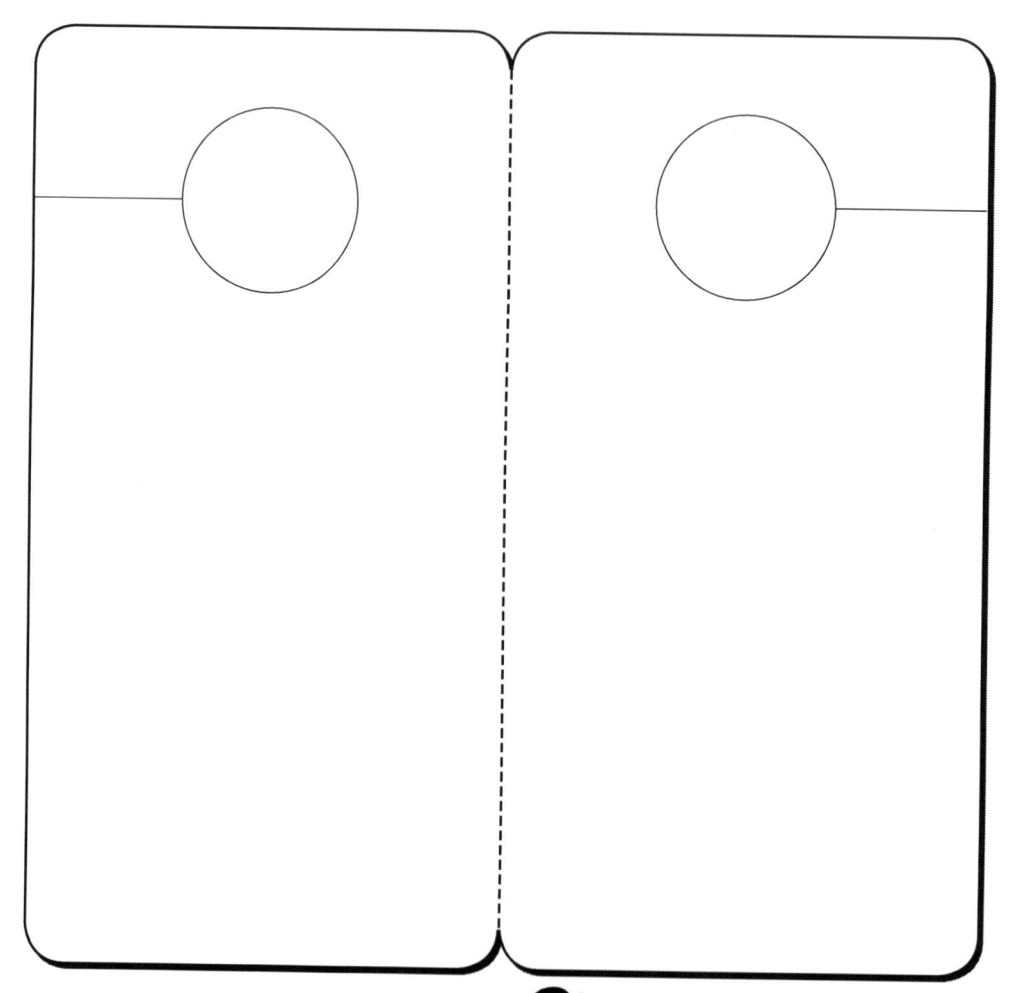

2) When you have finished your rough draft, get into groups. Each child should explain his/her door sign and the rest of the group should say what they think of it.

Suggest changes for others to make their door sign better!

SPEAKING AND LISTENING — 54

Prim-Ed Publishing   www.prim-ed.com

Do not disturb!

3 What did the group think of your sign?

Good ☐   Quite good ☐   Not good ☐

4 Is there anything you will change?

_____

_____

5 Complete your door sign. Do your best! Cut it out and hang it on your bedroom door!

SCHOOL IN THE PAST

TEACHERS NOTES

Objective: Interview an older family friend/member and report findings to the class.

Activities covered

- **Homework** – asking a family member/friend about their school days
- Recording and discussing information gathered

Background information

This lesson focuses on recounting information; children will use descriptions of school years ago.

The aim is for the children to interview an adult and then relate the information gathered back to the class.

Before the lesson

Children must be given time to complete their homework.

Provide children with suggestions and ideas for holding interviews.

The lesson (Pages 58 and 59)

Before giving the sheet for homework, read through all the questions that the children have to ask. (Allow no discussion at this time.)

Explain to the children that when they are conducting their 'interview', the interviewer and interviewee should be sitting down in a quiet place. Tell children they should choose a time when the family friend/member is not busy. Children should write down answers to the questions during the interview, otherwise they might forget them!

Children complete the sheet for homework by asking questions of an adult friend or relative.

Children can evaluate their interview by giving it a rating.

Have an informal class discussion, with children reporting back their findings.

Answers

Teacher check

Additional activities

Children look at a process—for example, how crisps are made—and answer questions in pairs.

Children look at a comic strip and answer questions in pairs.

Children use feely bags in group work – children must write a description of each object and then reveal the contents once all objects have been described. Can the children match their descriptions to the objects?

Children listen to a story/poem as told or read by the teacher. Children must retell it in their own words.

Children can make a 'School in the past' display in the classroom.

Have a class discussion on schools in the past.

Children can recount poems that have a storyline; for example, *The great detective* by Kit Wright or *With bells on* by Gervase Phinn.

The teacher can read the poem below to the class. Children can retell it and answer questions about it.

Early or late?

Oh, no! I'm very, very late,
I should be at school!
My alarm clock must be broken!
I'll look like such a fool!

I have to get ready really quick!
Where is my uniform?
It must be in the laundry bin!
It's dirty and it's worn!

I'm starving! Let me grab some food,
Oh, crumpets, there's no bread!
I can't seem to find my shoes!
I have a pounding head!

Oh, everything is going wrong!
It'll be a bad, bad day!
Then Mum says, 'You're up early,
On this sunny Saturday!'

SPEAKING AND LISTENING

Prim-Ed Publishing   www.prim-ed.com

TEACHERS NOTES

TELL THEM ABOUT IT!

Objective: Listen to other children describe experiences and ask questions about their reactions to them.

Activities covered

- Answering questions about personal experience in writing
- Orally describing experience
- Answering questions about personal experience orally
- Asking questions about other children's experiences

Background information

This lesson allows children to describe experiences they have had.

Children also have to listen quietly to the experiences of others and ask them questions about their experience.

Children needn't be describing mind-blowing experiences. If they cannot think of anything, a special birthday, Christmas, a new pet etc. will do.

Before the lesson

The teacher must relate an experience he/she has had to the class. This doesn't have to be too personal. It could be about someone the teacher knows. Be prepared to answer questions about this experience.

The lesson (Pages 60 and 61)

The teacher relates an experience to the class, telling the children first that they must think of questions to ask.

Children ask questions about the experience.

Children answer questions on the copymaster about an experience they have had.

Children relate this experience orally to the class.

The class asks questions about it, including questions about the child's feelings about the experience.

The child writes down how many of the class members' questions he/she answered.

Answers

Teacher check

Additional activities

Children can talk about their best day ever/their first day at school etc. and the class can ask them questions about it.

The teacher can have examples of poetry that tells of a child's experience; for example, *Grime and punishment* by Stephen Clarke.

Children can read the following poem about a child's experience and decide what questions they would like to ask the child.

Bathtime

My mother had delivered,
an enormous white machine.
This was not the Whirlpool™ kind,
it was to make *kids* clean.

'Put on your mask and get inside,'
said my mother very calmly.
I really felt very afraid,
I thought that she'd gone barmy!

I put on the oxygen mask,
this was to give me air.
I thought, 'This is outrageous!'
But to gripe I didn't dare.

Mum placed me right inside the tub,
She had a huge big smile.
She threw in some detergent,
and then she flicked the dial.

The machine went spinning round and round,
it really was quite fun.
I gurgled, splashed and sploshed about,
until the wash was done.

'You smell so beautifully fresh!' she said,
and tossed me in with her frocks.
She hung me on the washing line,
among the shirts and socks.

SPEAKING AND LISTENING

School in the past

1. Homework

Ask an adult family member/friend what school was like in his or her day when they were your age. Ask the following questions and write down the answers.

School was quite different years ago. I don't think you would have enjoyed it!

(a) What year was it?

(b) Who was your teacher?

(c) What time did you start and finish school?

Start

Finish

(d) What did you do at break time?

(e) Did you have these at school? (Tick the items you had.)

- desks
- marker pens
- posters
- curtains/blinds
- televisions
- blackboards
- buses
- CD players
- heating
- computers
- a library
- school bag

(f) Did you have a school uniform?

(g) If yes, what did you have to wear?

Page 1

58 SPEAKING AND LISTENING

Prim-Ed Publishing   www.prim-ed.com

School in the past

(h) Did you get much homework?

(i) What kind of homework did you get?
_____
_____
_____

(j) What was the best thing about school?
_____
_____
_____

(k) What was the worst thing about school?
_____
_____
_____

(l) What happened to children who were naughty?
_____
_____
_____

(m) Do you think school was better then or now?

(n) Why?
_____
_____
_____

Page 2

2) How did the interview go? (5 = excellent)

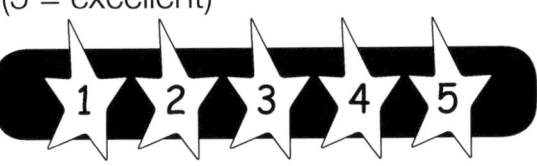

1   2   3   4   5

3) Tell the class what you found out.

Did you know?
In Borneo, children were considered old enough to go to school if they could reach an arm over their heads and touch the opposite ear!

SPEAKING AND LISTENING

Tell them about it!

1 (a) What happened?

Think about something that has happened to you—good or bad—and answer these questions.

_____

_____

_____

_____

_____

_____

_____

_____

_____

(b) When did it happen?

_____

_____

(c) How did it happen?

_____

_____

_____

_____

Tell them about it!

(d) Where did it happen?

_____

_____

(e) Was it a good or bad experience?   Good ☐   Bad ☐

(f) Who was there?

_____

_____

(g) What happened afterwards?

_____

_____

_____

_____

_____

2) Tell the class about your experience.

The class will ask you questions about your experience.

3) How many of the class members' questions did you answer? ☐

*Remember!
Questions often start with the words:
When? Why? Where? Who? What?*

SPEAKING AND LISTENING

GIVE ALL THE DETAILS!

TEACHERS NOTES

Objective: Become increasingly explicit in relation to people, places, times, processes and events by adding elaborative detail to what he/she describes and narrates.

Activities covered

- Adding detail to simple statements, as a class and individually
- **Pair work** – children have conversation using all question headings

Background information

Adding details such as where, when, why things happened, who was there etc. make sentences and conversation more interesting. Simply telling children to make their writing more interesting is too broad a request.

The headings *When? Who? Why? Where? What?* can be used to give children guidelines on how to add details. They can be placed on display in the classroom so that when the children are writing they can refer to them. Explain to children that not every heading will be used every time.

Before the lesson

The teacher must have examples ready to be completed on the board.

The class will be divided into pairs

The lesson (Pages 64 and 65)

The teacher gives examples of how we can add details to our writing and conversation. One example should be completed on the board to remind children how to add details.

Explain to the children they are going to use the headings *When? Who? Why? Where? What?*; for example, I went to town. When did I go? Who did I go with? Why did I go? Where in town did I go? What did I do there? This information can then all be placed together: 'I went to town, on Friday, with my brother, to find a new Playstation™ game. We went to Argos but they were all sold out!' It is possible that the end result will be more than one sentence.

As a class, children give ideas for Question 1 on their copymaster. Children write their answers.

Individually, children complete Question 2. Various answers can then be read to the class.

Pair work – Children tell their partners about an experience they have recently had, using all the headings.

Children assess their conversation.

Still in pairs, children read the short passage and, using arrows, show which questions are being answered.

Answers

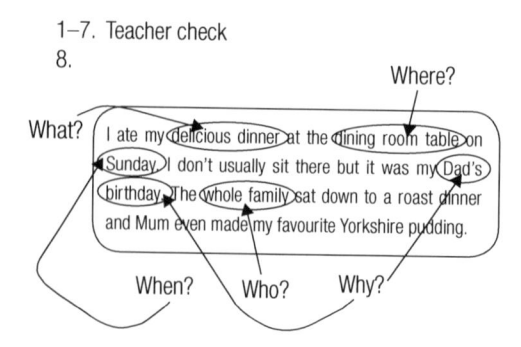

1–7. Teacher check

8.

What? — I ate my delicious dinner at the dining room table on Sunday. I don't usually sit there but it was my Dad's birthday. The whole family sat down to a roast dinner and Mum even made my favourite Yorkshire pudding.

Where? — dining room table
When? — Sunday
Who? — whole family
Why? — Dad's birthday

Additional activities

Children write a few lines on a given subject. Children add details as described and rewrite their lines of text, adding the details.

SPEAKING AND LISTENING

TEACHERS NOTES

ASK IT!

Objective: Listen to and read fiction and non-fiction texts and ask questions about them.

Activities covered

- Asking questions (orally)
- Reading excerpt, asking questions (as a class)
- **Pair work** – asking questions about adverts
- Discussing all questions with the class

Background information

This lesson gives children the opportunity to listen to what they are hearing and formulate questions based on what they've heard. Children must be told to think, while they are listening, of questions they would like to ask.

Before the lesson

Have ready a short story or similar that can be told/read to the class and about which they can ask questions.

The class will be divided into pairs.

The lesson (Pages 66 and 67)

The teacher tells the class about something, or reads a story or poem about which questions can be asked.

The class listens to the teacher and formulates questions.

On his/her copymaster, each child writes two questions he/she would like to ask.

Children ask the teacher questions about what they've just heard.

As a class, read through the excerpt in Question 2 and formulate two questions.

Pair work – Look at the adverts. Formulate two questions about each.

Answers

1–2. Teacher check
3. Answer will vary, but could include:
   Where were they going? Why did they have to go away? Why did John stay behind?
4. Answer will vary, but could include:
   What breed are the puppies? How much do they cost? How old are they? Are they male or female? How many are there? What is the address?
5. Answer will vary, but could include:
   When is football practice? Where is football practice held? When will matches be? Will I need to provide my own football kit? Do you need a goalkeeper? Who will coach us?

Additional activities

Listen to stories told by children about their favourite holidays. Other children ask questions.

Listen to a poem being read and children ask questions; for example, *Asking questions* by Gervase Phinn or *Where do all the teachers go?* by Peter Dixon.

Have a class discussion on when in life we ask questions.

SPEAKING AND LISTENING

Give all the details!

1) Make this statement more interesting by adding details.

Adding details makes sentences more interesting!

Answer these questions: When? Where? Who? Why? What?

I went to visit a friend.

___

2) Make this statement more interesting by adding details.

Answer these questions: When? Where? Who? Why? What?

I watched TV.

___

3) Read your interesting statements out to the class!

SPEAKING AND LISTENING

Give all the details!

4) Tell your partner about something you experienced last week. Don't forget to add all the details!

5) Was your conversation full of details? [yes] [no]

6) Listen while your partner tells you something he/she experienced last week.

7) Was your partner's conversation full of details? [yes] [no]

8) Still in pairs, read these sentences. Draw arrows to show which question each part of the text is answering.

What? **Where?**

> I ate my delicious dinner at the dining room table on Sunday. I don't usually sit there but it was my Dad's birthday. The whole family sat down to a roast dinner and Mum even made my favourite Yorkshire pudding.

When? **Why?**

Who?

Ask it!

We ask questions when we want to find out something. What questions might you ask in a normal day?

1 Listen to the teacher. Write two questions you would like to ask.

(a) _____   (b) _____

2 Ask the questions!

As a class, read these sentences together.

> I didn't want to be away for Christmas and Mum knew this! I wanted to wake up on Christmas morning, run downstairs and find the present with my name on it! Why did we have to go? Would I be able to change my Mum's mind? It wasn't fair that John could stay behind!

3 Write down two questions you would like to ask about these sentences.

(a) _____   (b) _____

SPEAKING AND LISTENING

Ask it!

4) Work with a partner. Look at the puppy advert below. Write two questions you would need to ask before buying a puppy.

(a) _____   (b) _____

_____   _____

_____   _____

_____   _____

Don't be afraid to ask questions!

Puppies for sale! Call 789456

Under 9s football team needs new players. Call 987321

5) Work with a partner. Look at the football advert above. Write two questions you would need to ask before joining a football team.

(a) _____   (b) _____

_____   _____

_____   _____

_____   _____

SPEAKING AND LISTENING

WHAT'S YOUR OPINION?

TEACHERS NOTES

Objective: Engage in real and imaginary situations involving language use.

Activities covered

- As a class, discussing given topic and formulating their own opinions
- Writing opinions on copymaster
- **Group work** – sharing opinions with group
- Role-playing

Background information

This lesson focuses firstly on a real situation, with children giving their own opinions on various things, and justifying their opinions. The children are then placed in an imaginary scene where they have to role-play a given situation. Both of these activities involve a particular type of language use. As this objective concentrates on language use, almost any real or imaginary scene can be created in which children role-play the situation. Other areas of the curriculum can be incorporated here, such as acting out a scene from history or demonstrating something from science.

Before the lesson

Have ready a topic for discussion, where children will give their own opinions; for example, fast food, wearing school uniforms, having TV banned.

The class will be divided into groups.

The lesson (Pages 70 and 71)

Have a class discussion on the teacher's chosen topic.

Children give their own opinions of the topic and the teacher writes some of them on the board. It is important that children say why they have that opinion. For example: 'I don't like fast foods' is not sufficient – 'I don't like fast foods because they don't taste natural' is better.

On their copymaster, children write their opinions of various things.

Group work – Each item is chosen, one by one, and each child gets the chance to voice his/her opinion and say why he/she feels that way. Do tell the children that they must have respect for other children's opinions! Children sort items according to whether their group held the same opinions on them.

Group work – Children role-play an imaginary situation and assess their work.

Answers

Teacher check

Additional activities

Role-play common arguments between classmates.

Role-play safety issues, such as not talking to strangers.

The children can create a display in the classroom on 'What we think of school'.

Children suggest ideas on how their own school could be improved.

SPEAKING AND LISTENING

Prim-Ed Publishing   www.prim-ed.com

TEACHERS NOTES

WHAT IS IT LIKE TO BE A TEACHER?

Objective: Ask questions that will satisfy his/her curiosity and wonder.

Activities covered

- Asking teacher questions
- Formulating questions to ask people in different occupations
- **Pair work** – role-play interviews

Background information

Children are by nature curious and they love to ask questions. This lesson gives them freedom to ask questions of the teacher and also to find things out for themselves.

Remind children that questions in this lesson must relate to the person's job, where applicable, and not his/her personal life.

Before the lesson

Be prepared for the questions!

The class will be divided into pairs.

The lesson (Pages 72 and 73)

Children are reminded about how a question will often begin, using the prompts at the bottom of the first copymaster.

Children write on their copymaster one question that they would like to ask the teacher about his/her job.

Children ask the teacher questions. If one child has the same question as another child, they can both just fill in the answer.

Children write down the teacher's answer.

Children write one question they could ask of people in different occupations and imagine their reply.

Pair work – Children role-play interviews with the list of people in Questions 7 and 8, taking turns to be the interviewer and interviewee. (Obviously many answers will have to be made up!)

Answers

1–2. Teacher check
3. Answers will vary, but could include:
   What do you do if a child is terrified of you?
4. Teacher check
5. Answers will vary, but could include:
   Do you know how many bricks to order before you start building?
6. Teacher check
7. Answers will vary, but could include:
   (a) Does it hurt when someone throws you down?
   (b) Have you ever kissed a frog and have it turn into a prince?
   (c) Do you really enjoy playing fetch?
   (d) What is the most expensive thing you've bought?
   (e) What is your favourite magic spell?
   (f) Are you scared of spiders?
8–9. Teacher check

Additional activities

Play a game. Each child gets the chance to choose an occupation, and the rest of the class must ask questions to find out what his/her occupation is. The answers to the questions may only be 'yes' and 'no'.

Children can read non-fiction books that answer questions; for example, *'Tell me why'* books. Questions could include: Does space ever stop? What makes popcorn pop? What makes stars shine? Where does the wind come from? Why do we shiver? Why is my hair darker when it's wet? Questions and answers can be displayed.

SPEAKING AND LISTENING

What's your opinion?

1) What do you think of the following?

'Opinion' means what you think of something!

(a) television

(b) books

(c) sweets

(d) cheese

(e) school

(f) boats

(g) rainy days

(h) homework

(i) music

What's your opinion?

You should always listen to and respect what others have to say!

2) Tell your group your ideas on the items in Question 1. Tell your group why you feel this way!

(a) Colour the items your group had the same opinions on in blue.

(b) Colour the items your group had different opinions on in red.

- television
- books
- sweets
- cheese
- school
- boats
- rainy days
- homework
- music

3) In your groups, each person must take a turn to explain to the teacher (the rest of the group) why his or her homework is not done!

(a) What did the group think of your explanation?

Very good   Good   Fair

(b) How could you have made your explanation better?

_____

_____

_____

_____

We think school is fun!

SPEAKING AND LISTENING

What is it like to be a teacher?

1) What question would you like to ask your teacher about his/her job?

Have you ever wondered what it's like to be a teacher?

_____

_____

2) What was your teacher's answer? _____

_____

Have you ever wondered what it's like to be a doctor?

3) What question would you like to ask a doctor about his/her job?

_____

_____

4) What do you think a doctor would reply? _____

_____

5) What question would you like to ask a builder about his/her job?

Have you ever wondered what it's like to be a builder?

_____

_____

6) What do you think a builder would reply? _____

_____

Remember!
Questions often start with:

Who?   What?   When?   Why?   Where?   What if?   How?

---

72   SPEAKING AND LISTENING   Prim-Ed Publishing   www.prim-ed.com

What is it like to be a teacher?

7) What question would you ask each of the following?

(a) A champion wrestler _____

(b) A princess _____

(c) A dog _____

(d) A millionaire _____

(e) Harry Potter _____

(f) Spider-man™ _____

8) Choose two more people. Write their names and a question you would like to ask each.

(a) [_____] (b) [_____]

9) Work with a partner. Role-play interviews with the above people.

Remember: If you are ever unsure about something, just ask!

SPEAKING AND LISTENING

YESTERDAY

TEACHERS NOTES

Objective: Develop comprehension strategies, recalling details and events, assimilating facts and retelling stories.

Activities covered

- Answering questions about the day before
- Discussing answers with the class
- As a class, writing three remembered facts
- Researching facts, orally telling facts, listening to facts and retelling facts in writing

Background information

It is best not to do this lesson on a Monday so that the previous day at school is not too far in the past. This lesson focuses on recalling details and the children should have some fun recalling details about the previous day. The teacher will also have to remember!

Before the lesson

The teacher can have ready a list of facts learnt in the last week in the subjects of science, history and geography (for Question 3 on the copymaster).

The teacher will need to choose a topic for Question 4. This could be related to work being completed in other subject areas. Non-fiction books on the topic will need to be available for the children's research.

The lesson (Pages 76 and 77)

Children answer the questions on their copymaster, giving details about the previous day. It is important that children answer these questions with no discussion at this point at all.

Once all children have answered as many questions as they can, they fill in how many questions they answered.

Have a class discussion on the questions and answers for Question 1.

As a class, children think of one fact learnt in each of the mentioned subjects in the last week. Children need to write only one fact on their sheet for each subject in Question 3.

The teacher should tell the children the topic that has been chosen for Question 4.

Children will need to use non-fiction books to research, choose and write one fact about the topic.

Children must take it in turns to share their facts with the rest of the class.

Once all the facts have been discussed, children should write a paragraph of factual text about the topic on their copymaster.

Answers

Teacher check

Additional activities

Children can ask someone in their family what they were like as a baby. Children can tell the class, perhaps bringing a photo.

Children can ask older family members about their own childhood and report back to the class with the stories.

Children can recall events such as their last birthday/Christmas and tell their group about it.

SPEAKING AND LISTENING

Prim-Ed Publishing   www.prim-ed.com

TEACHERS NOTES

READ A BOOK

Objective: Express a more formal response by giving a considered personal opinion of a book in oral or written form.

Activities covered

- Reading a book
- Reviewing a book – written and oral

Background information

Children will have to read an entire fiction book for this lesson. This can be a daunting task for those who have difficulty reading. For such children, allow them to choose a simple and short book, perhaps one from the younger classes.

Before the lesson

The children will need to read a whole book from start to finish, but the book needn't be long. Make sure that children who have chosen easier books are not teased by the others. Give sufficient time for children to read their book.

The lesson (Pages 78 and 79)

Children read a book.

The teacher can read through the copymaster with the children so that they know what is expected of them.

Children complete their book review on their copymaster.

Children tell the class about their book, and whether they would recommend it or not.

Children rate their book, and their talk.

Answers

Teacher check

Additional activities

Children give scores to books/articles/passages that have been read in class. Rating can be completed using different headings, such as interest, storyline, pictures, humour etc.

Look at a known publisher's website to see what books are new, and read book reviews.

Mention well-known children's authors in the UK.

Look at *www.ukchildrensbooks.co.uk* for some great links to children's publishers.

SPEAKING AND LISTENING

Yesterday

1. Think about yesterday. Read these questions and answer as many as you can!

    (a) What subject did you do first? _____

    (b) Write one thing you learned during the day. _____

    (c) What did you eat for your lunch? _____

    (d) What did you do at break time? _____

    (e) Was anyone absent? [yes] [no]
    Who? _____

    (f) What was the teacher wearing? _____

    (g) What was the weather like? _____

    (h) What colour socks were you wearing? _____

    (i) Did the class get into trouble? [yes] [no]

    (j) What subject did you do after the lunch break? _____

2. (a) How many questions could you answer out of 10? [ ]

    (b) Discuss your answers with the class.

SPEAKING AND LISTENING

Yesterday

3 As a class, try to remember one fact you learned in the last week for each of these subjects:

Science _____

Geography _____

History _____

I've forgotten what I was going to say!

4 (a) Our topic to research is:

_____

(b) Write one fact about the topic.

_____

_____

(c) Listen to all the facts. Use the facts to write some sentences about the topic.

_____
_____
_____
_____
_____
_____
_____
_____

SPEAKING AND LISTENING 77

Read a book

1 Read a book and complete the following review.

Title of book	
Author	
Plot (story)	The book is about ...
Characters	
Does the book have pictures?	

Read a book

Write one sentence about the book.	
What is your favourite part of the book and why?	
What is your least favourite part of the book and why?	
Rate your book with a score out of 10	★★★★★★

2) Tell the class about your book!

Rate your talk with a score out of 10

★★★★★★★★★★

Did you know? The Oxford English dictionary, *first published in 1884, took 22 years to write!*

Remember! Reading is knowledge!

SPEAKING AND LISTENING 79

CAN YOU REMEMBER?

TEACHERS NOTES

Objective: Describe everyday experiences, events and objects.

Activities covered
- Answering questions about weekend in writing
- **Pair work** – telling partner about weekend
- Describing an object – in writing and orally
- Listening to descriptions given by other children

Background information
The aim of this lesson is to describe ordinary everyday objects and events, and to describe them in as interesting a way as possible.

Before the lesson
Children must take note of weekend details.

Ensure there are lots of interesting objects in the classroom for children to describe. Teachers will need to chose an object to describe, as an example to the children.

The lesson (Pages 82 and 83)
The teacher goes through the questions on the first copymaster to make sure that children understand them.

Children fill in details about their weekend.

Pair work – Children describe their weekend to their partner, trying to make it sound as interesting as possible!

Before completing the second copymaster, the teacher should choose an item in the classroom to describe, using the headings; for example, a tap (*shape:* rounded, straight, stem, *size:* 10–15 cm tall, thin, *colour:* silver, shiny, *use:* washing hands, making a glass of orange squash, *feel:* cold or hot, slippery, metallic, *anything else:* dripping, has limescale).

Children have to guess the name of the object.

Children choose a different classroom object. Taking care not to let other children see what they have written, they brainstorm words to describe their object on their sheet, underneath each heading.

Children take it in turns to describe their object to the group. The group has to guess what the object is.

Children rate their description by colouring the stars.

Answers
Teacher check

Additional activities
Children describe their day so far.

Children explain what they had for dinner the previous night, and see if they can remember their meals for the last five days.

Read poems about everyday things; for example, *Things I have been doing lately* by Allen Ahlberg, or:

> **Friday afternoon**
>
> I don't care what you say to me,
> because it's Friday afternoon.
> You can call me all sorts of funny names,
> this feeling you can't ruin.
>
> You can make me eat cabbage and mince,
> I'll even wash my plate.
> I'll pretend the mean neighbour
> is my very best mate.
>
> I'll tidy my entire room,
> I'll clean the hamster's cage.
> If you tell me to, I'll brush my hair,
> and I don't require a wage.
>
> You can play with all my favourite games,
> you can keep the TV's remote.
> I'll be kind to my bratty sister,
> I'll hang up my winter coat.
>
> Yes, nothing can push me down today,
> I could jump right over the moon.
> You'll find me willing and cheerful,
> on this Friday afternoon.

SPEAKING AND LISTENING

Prim-Ed Publishing   www.prim-ed.com

TEACHERS NOTES

HOW DO YOU FEEL?

Objective: Express feelings in order to clarify them and explain them to others.

Activities covered

- Having a class discussion
- Answering questions on the copymaster
- Expressing feelings

Background information

The aim of this lesson is to present children with different scenarios and to get them to express and identify their feelings. In order to think about their feelings, they must first put them in written form and then share them with others. It must be stressed that no teasing is allowed and children are not allowed to laugh at other people's fears etc.

Before the lesson

Have ideas for discussion on feelings.

The class will be divided into groups.

The lesson (Pages 84 and 85)

Have a class discussion about different feelings; for example, jealousy, love, anger, sadness, anxiety, boredom, excitement.

Children answer questions on the copymaster about how people might be feeling in different situations.

Children complete the sentences and draw pictures to explain when they have different feelings.

Group work – Discuss answers in the group, each having a turn to give his/her ideas.

Answers

1. Answer will vary, but could include:
   (a) sad, disappointed
   (b) upset, sad, angry
   (c) excited, happy
   (d) guilty, sad, worried
   (e) jealous, angry
   (f) scared, frightened, upset
2–3. Teacher check

Additional activities

Each child gets a different card, and each card has a different feeling written on it. Children take a few minutes to think about their 'feeling' and then tell the class when they have had that feeling before.

Discuss different fears, such as arachnophobia (fear of spiders), bibliophobia (fear of books), pedophobia (fear of children), hippophobia (fear of horses) and hyrophobia (fear of water).

Children can draw faces showing different emotions, label the faces and display them in the classroom.

The class can look at 'emoticons' on the Internet – faces used in emails to show different emotions. The teacher should check whether the content is suitable before allowing the children access.

Children read poems about different feelings; for example, *Under my bed* by Steve Turner, *Starting school* by Steve Turner and *I'm not scared* by Gervase Phinn.

SPEAKING AND LISTENING

Can you remember?

1) Complete this table about your last weekend.

Name one place you went to.	
Name two people you saw.	
Name one programme you watched on television.	
Name one meal you ate.	
What was the weather like?	
Did you go to any shops? Name one if you did.	yes no
Did you speak to anyone on the phone? Who?	yes no
What time did you go to bed on Saturday night?	
Was it a good or bad weekend? Say why.	good bad

2) How many questions out of nine could you answer? ☐

3) Tell your partner about your weekend, using the ideas you wrote down. Try to make your weekend sound interesting!

Did you know? Our memories are most closely linked to smells!

SPEAKING AND LISTENING

Can you remember?

4 (a) Choose one object that you can see.

(b) Write the name of your object. _____

(Do not let anyone see this!)

5 Write words under each heading to describe your object.

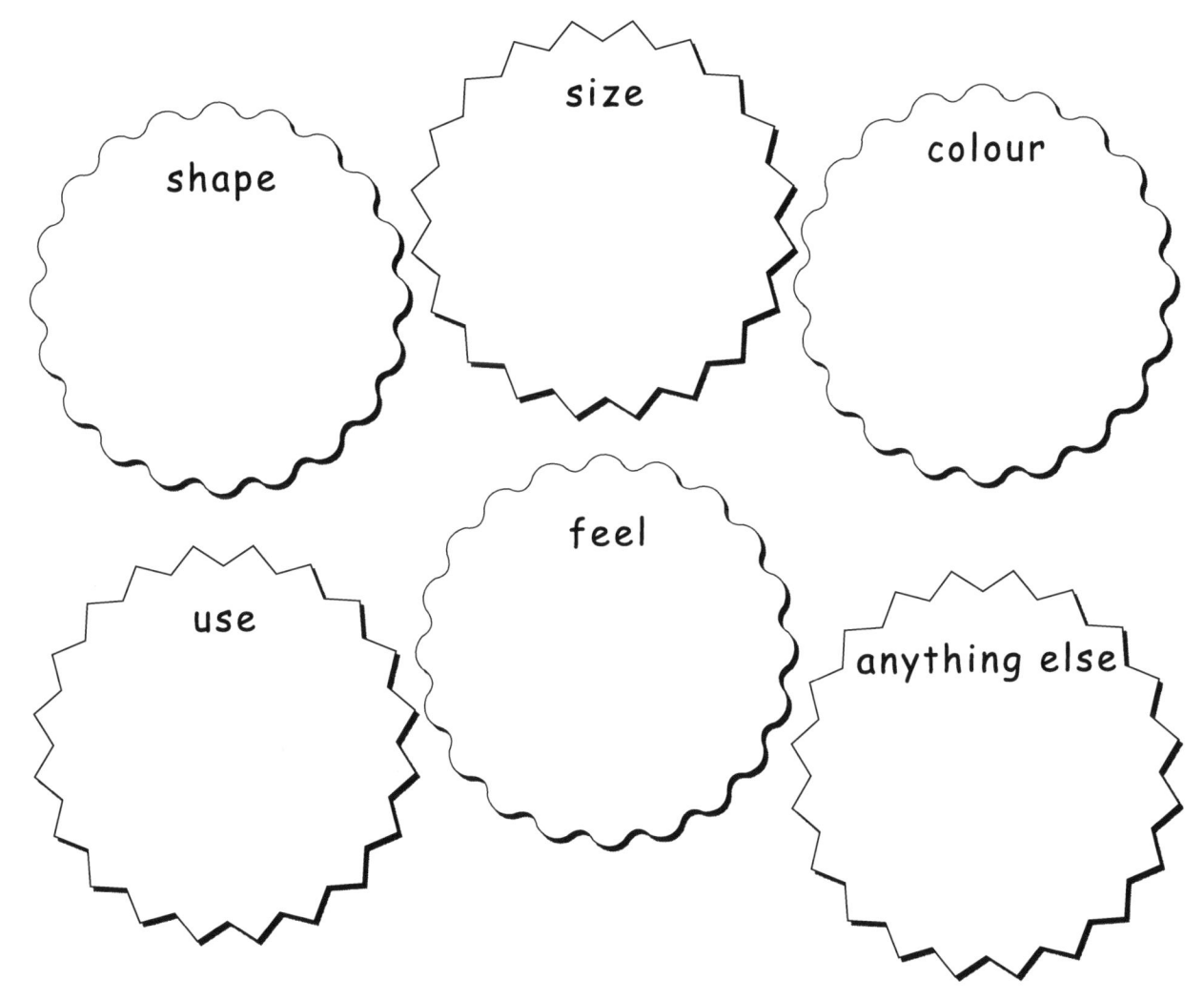

- shape
- size
- colour
- use
- feel
- anything else

6 (a) Describe your object to the group.

(b) Did your group guess your object?

yes   no

(c) Colour the stars to rate your description out of five.

SPEAKING AND LISTENING

How do you feel?

1 How do you think these people might be feeling?

(a) Pat is looking forward to going to the animal farm, but it is raining.

Feelings are something we all have. Sometimes we might be happy, or sad, or angry or bored.

(b) Ahmed's favourite cousin is going to live in America.

(c) Jane is going on holiday to Spain.

(d) Peter borrowed his brother's CD player and broke it.

(e) Sunita's sister receives more pocket money than Sunita.

(f) Orla does not like dogs, but is chased by one while walking to school.

We blink more often when we are tired, bored, angry, embarrassed or worried.

SPEAKING AND LISTENING

Prim-Ed Publishing   www.prim-ed.com

How do you feel?

Remember to always respect the feelings of others!

2 Complete the sentences and draw pictures to show your feelings.

(a) I am happy when _____

(b) I am sad when _____

(c) I am angry when _____

(d) I am scared when _____

3 Discuss your answers in your group. Each person must get a chance to give his or her answers!

SPEAKING AND LISTENING

TELL A STORY

TEACHERS NOTES

Objective: Tell stories in his/her own words and answer questions about them.

Activities covered

- Completing a story
- Reading story to group
- Evaluating others' work
- Answering questions about a story

Background information

The children will be able to write stories with some guidelines to make it easier. Children must be clear in their minds about their storyline before they begin writing – something sad/happy/exciting etc. must happen in their story; in other words, it must be a story worth telling! The passage with blanks must be read beforehand, as a class, and children must start thinking about ideas as it's being read, asking and answering their own questions in their head, as to what will happen in the story. Stress to children that before beginning a writing task they should think first! Give children 'thinking time'.

Before the lesson

The class will be divided into groups.

The lesson (Pages 88 and 89)

The teacher reads through the passage and tells children that they must start to think about the story.

The teacher gives the children 'thinking time'.

Children fill in the blanks to tell their story.

Group work – Children read their story to the group, who then comment and, as a group, give the child a grade.

Explain to children that if they received a weak grade, they should not be upset, but rather try to improve on it! (If a child gets particularly bad reviews, step in and look for something positive!)

Children answer questions about their story.

Answers

1. Answers will vary, but story could read:

   Once upon a time, there was a boy called <u>Prince Horrid</u> who lived in a big <u>castle.</u> He loved to play in the <u>muddy river</u> and he went there every day after <u>dinner.</u> One day, a <u>river monster</u> appeared. The <u>monster</u> asked the boy to help him. He said he needed to <u>find his child.</u> So the boy went <u>calling around the river, searching under stones and in the reeds</u>, and the <u>monster watched from the water, which he could not leave.</u> Then, the <u>boy heard a tiny cry, not too far from the shore. He went searching and found a tiny river monster, shivering and frightened. He had been picked up by an eagle and simply dropped when the eagle didn't fancy the taste of him. The boy gently picked up the little monster and returned him to the water. The river monster was very grateful and, from that day on, the prince and monster became firm friends. Whenever the prince went to the river to play, the monster watched over him.</u>

2 – 4. Teacher check

Additional activities

Children write stories on a computer, print and display them.

Children tell favourite stories to the class and the class asks questions.

In groups, children retell in their own words stories that the teacher has read.

Read folktales and answer questions about them.

Discuss with the class ancient storytellers in the UK.

Read poems that tell a story; for example, *School* by Steve Turner.

Look at Hans Christian Andersen's fairytales on the Internet. A good website is *www.andersenfairytales.com*

SPEAKING AND LISTENING

Prim-Ed Publishing   www.prim-ed.com

TEACHERS NOTES

READING IS FUN!

Objective: Listen to, read, learn and recite a varied and appropriate repertoire of rhymes and poems.

Activities covered

- Choosing a poem to recite and writing it down
- Learning a poem, thinking about appropriate expression and/or actions
- Reciting poem to the class
- Reading given poem aloud
- Drawing pictures to go with the poem
- Identifying rhyming words in the poem

Background information

There are so many rhymes and poems that could be used here. Those that are humorous will grab the children's attention, so keep the choice light-hearted and funny. Books can sometimes be daunting, especially for less able children, but poetry is mostly shorter and easier to read. Poetry should play a leading role in the teaching of language and although children may groan at the thought of studying poetry, once they see that poetry can be funny and enjoyable, it will open their minds up. Then, later, the teacher can move onto more serious poetry. Children should be encouraged to read poetry with expression.

Before the lesson

Children choose a poem or part of a poem to learn off by heart. The poem should be about 4–8 lines long. Time must be given for children to learn it.

The teacher should assist children in choosing a poem.

Have ready examples of other poems that can be read for enjoyment. The teacher should demonstrate reading a poem with expression and actions.

The lesson (Pages 90 and 91)

Children choose, learn and practise their poem/part of poem. Children think about how to recite their poem with expression and actions.

Children recite their poem to the class. (If children are reciting part of a poem, they can read the rest of it, so that children hear the whole poem.)

Have a brief class discussion on the different poems.

Children choose which poem they liked best out of the those they heard.

The class read the given poem aloud, as a class.

Children draw pictures to go with the poem.

Children identify rhyming words in the poem.

Answers

1–4. Teacher check
5. year/fear, hair/underwear, pen/ten, sweet/feet, old/mould

Additional activities

The class can recite their poem to others/visitors in the school.

The whole class can recite a poem together, one with actions would work well.

Children read through and recite common nursery rhymes.

Children do actions with poems and rhymes.

Children read entertaining poems such as *Dear Gran* by Trevor Harvey, *Do I talk in my sleep?* by Steve Turner, *Please Mrs Butler* by Allen Ahlberg and *Nativity play* by Gervase Phinn.

Children look at poetry websites; for example,
www.gigglepoetry.com
www.poetry4kids.com
and
www.shadowpoetry.com/links/childrenspoetrylinks.html

Children look at poetry written by other children. Examples can be found on the website:
www.dreamagic.com/poetry/children.html

SPEAKING AND LISTENING

Tell a story

1) Read the following story and complete it by filling in the blank spaces.

Once upon a time, there was a boy called _____

who lived in a big _____. He loved to play in the

_____ and he went there every day after

_____.

One day, a _____ appeared. The

_____ asked the boy to help him. He said

he needed to _____.

So the boy _____

_____ and the

_____.

Then _____

_____

_____

_____

_____

_____.

2) Read your story to your group.

3) Colour the grade your group gave your story.

A	B	C	D	E
excellent	very good	good	fair	needs work

Remember! Always read through your work when you are finished!

Tell a story

4 Answer the questions about your story.

(a) Draw and label the two main characters.

(b) Where is the story set?

_____

_____

(c) What is the most important event?

_____

_____

_____

(d) Which is your favourite part?

_____

_____

_____

Reading is fun!

1) Choose a poem or part of a poem to learn off by heart.

Write the poem here.

_____
_____
_____
_____
_____
_____
_____
_____

2) Think about how you could recite your poem with:

(a) expression	(b) action

3) (a) Recite your poem to the class.

(b) Did you remember all the words?

[yes] [no]

Reading is fun!

4) Read this poem aloud and draw pictures to go with it.

Schoolbag

Today I cleaned my school bag,
I hadn't done it all year.
I wondered what lurked at the bottom,
I felt a little fear.

I took out all my schoolbooks,
And some long and frizzy hair.
Some dirty, crumpled paper
And an item of underwear!

I found the BEYBLADE© I had lost,
And my favourite pen.
And there was my toy soldier,
I'd had since I was ten.

I found a furry sandwich,
And an old and sticky sweet.
There was something I couldn't identify,
Which honked like smelly feet!

My bag was like a junk shop,
Crammed with the new and old.
But I think I'll clean it more often,
To prevent the slime and mould.

Remember! Poems do not always rhyme!

5) Circle the rhyming words!

SPEAKING AND LISTENING

ACT IT OUT!

TEACHERS NOTES

Objective: Re-create stories and poems in improvisational drama.

Activities covered

- Reading poetry aloud as a class
- **Group work** – acting the poem out
- Answering questions about own performance

Background information

Poetry has been used in this lesson for children to act out. Children must use their imagination and the drama should be almost unrehearsed, with the group having just enough time to read through it, decide on how it will be acted out and make a few practice runs.

Before the lesson

The teacher can have ready other examples of poems that can be acted out.

The class will be divided into groups.

The lesson (Pages 94 and 95)

Children read through the given poem as a class.

Group work – Children read the poem together and decide how it will be acted out. One person should be the speaker. Children can write next to the poem the different roles and who is playing them.

Children act the poem out for the class.

Children answer questions on the copymaster about their performance.

Answers

Teacher check

Additional activities

The same lesson can be repeated with stories, especially stories that the children are familiar with, such as fairytales.

Children can change the endings of fairytales or nursery rhymes while acting.

In groups, children act out scenes from their favourite cartoons.

Look at drama in their local area and discuss nearby theatres.

Children can look at programmes for plays.

Children can watch a play in a theatre.

Children can read poems and act them out; for example, *Ghosts* by Kit Wright and *The car trip* by Michael Rosen.

SPEAKING AND LISTENING

Prim-Ed Publishing   www.prim-ed.com

TEACHERS NOTES

SET THE SCENE

Objective: Use play and improvisational drama to sustain imaginary situations.

Activities covered

- Brainstorm topic word as a class
- **Pair work** – having conversation on given topic
- Acting out beach scenes
- Assessing their performances

Background information

This lesson uses the beach as an imaginary situation but virtually any scene can be set; for example, outer space, park, school. Having a discussion before any drama takes place sets the scene and will hopefully give children ideas and help them to imagine the topic.

Before the lesson

The teacher can have ready a list of words that matches the topic, to add to children's own.

The class will be divided into pairs.

The lesson (Pages 96 and 97)

Have a class discussion about the beach and brainstorm 'beach' words.

Children write words that have something to do with the beach. Get them to write down their words first, and they can then add to their list with words from others.

Pair work – Children have a conversation about the beach, using all the words in their box.

Children assess their conversation – Did they use all their words? Was their conversation interesting?

Still in pairs, children act out scenes from the beach. Some of these can be performed for the whole class.

Children give themselves a score for each scenario.

Answers

1. Answers will vary, but include:
   sand dunes, waves, fish, shark, whale, dolphin, starfish, shells, crabs, beach ball, umbrella, towel, sunscreen, sunglasses, volleyball, bathing costume, sandcastle, bucket, spade, water, boats, ships, seagulls, sun, swimming, diving, salt, seaweed, fishing rod, tackle, hooks, bait, sunbathe, heat, splash, lifeguard, snorkel, surfboard etc.
2. – 5. Teacher check

Additional activities

Choose an imaginary place—for example, Snow White's cottage—or a real place—for example, under the sea—and complete the same activity as above.

In groups, children can draw rough comic strips of how a scene will be acted out, and then practise it and act it out in front of the class.

In groups or pairs, children can act out a chosen scene from an imaginary or real place and the class must guess the location.

SPEAKING AND LISTENING

Act it out!

Reading a poem is fun, but acting it out is even better!

Don't forget to use movement in your drama!

1. Read this poem as a class.

Next!

A waiting room is somewhere
you don't like to be.
At first you sit down and relax,
and see what you can see.

You look at all the posters
that are plastered on the wall.
It doesn't take too long
before you have read them all.

Your attention will then turn
to others sitting there,
some who look quite worried
and some without a care.

There's a man with a broken arm,
and a baby with a cold,
a mother trying hard to hush,
a child that's very bold.

There's a young chap with a bandaged foot,
and an old man with a stick,
a woman with some tattered nerves who
should see the doctor quick.

Now, you've looked at everything
there's nothing left to do.
Time stretches out before you,
and you begin to stew.

You really have to see the doctor,
your toenail is in pain,
but if you get up and flee the room,
you'll have to wait again.

So, you sit and look around you,
and outside at the trees,
waiting, hoping, praying,
for the joyous sound 'Next, please!'

2. Work as a group to act out this poem. One person in the group will read it while others do the acting!

94 SPEAKING AND LISTENING

Prim-Ed Publishing   www.prim-ed.com

Act it out!

③ Answer the questions about your role in the poem.

(a) What part did you play?
_____

(b) What was the best part of your group performance?
_____
_____

(c) How could your group performance be improved?
_____
_____

(d) Colour the stars to rate your group performance out of five.

☆☆☆☆☆

④ Draw yourself in your role.

Set the scene

1) In the box below, write words that have something to do with the beach.

_____ ☐	☐ _____
_____ ☐	☐ _____
_____ ☐	☐ _____
_____ ☐	☐ _____
_____ ☐	☐ _____
_____ ☐	☐ _____

2) In pairs, have a conversation about the beach, using all the words from the box above! Tick each word as you use it.

(a) Did you manage to use all the words? **yes** **no**

(b) Was your conversation interesting? **yes** **no**

Where is your closest beach?

Set the scene

3) Act out the following beach scenes with your partner.

Colour the stars to give yourselves a score out of five for each performance.

Is my fin so scary?

(a) A child stamps on your sandcastle.

(b) You see a shark's fin while swimming in the sea.

(c) A crab pinches you on a toe and someone gets the crab off for you.

(d) The lifeguard rescues someone from the big waves.

4) Tick your favourite performance.

(a) sandcastle ☐   (b) shark's fin ☐

(c) crab ☐   (d) lifeguard ☐

5) Why was this performance your favourite?

_____
_____
_____
_____

Prim-Ed Publishing   www.prim-ed.com   **SPEAKING AND LISTENING** **97**

SILLY STUFF!

TEACHERS NOTES

Objective: Listen to and say nonsense words and unusual words.

Activities covered

- As a class, completing examples of swapping letters around
- Deciphering sentences on the copymaster
- Making nonsense words by changing letters around
- **Group work** – nonsense rhyming words
- Writing nonsense sentences

Background information

This lesson uses children's basic knowledge of phonics and experiments with it! The lesson should be fun and enjoyable.

Before the lesson

The teacher must have examples ready to do with the class.

The class will be divided into groups.

The lesson (Pages 100 and 101)

The teacher gives examples to the class where letters in words are changed around; for example, The cat ate its food. – The fat ate its cood./The boy has a car. – The coy has a bar./The night is dark. – The dight is nark./The bird has a worm. – The wird has a borm. (Notice that only letters of nouns are being swapped around, otherwise it might all get a bit confusing!) The teacher must do quite a few examples with the class.

Children work out what the sentence should be (on the copymaster).

Children change letters of nouns around to make nonsense words.

Group work – Children make rhyming nonsense words and say them.

Children write two sentences with the letters changed around and their group must try to work out what they are. (Children should write the correct sentences first and then change these.)

Answers

1. (a) The dog wagged its tail. (b) The bed is soft.
   (c) The prince lost his crown. (d) The man ate a cake.
   (e) The horse jumped over the gate.
2. (a) The toy climbed the bree.
   (b) The ceacher was tross.
   (c) The little pirl ate a gear.
   (d) The buppy played with the pall.
   (e) The caddy drove the lar.
3 – 5. Teacher check

Additional activities

Read nonsense rhymes and poems; for example, *The Squirdle*, *Ning Nang Nong* and *The Werkling* by Spike Milligan, *Hot sizzling lips* by Paul Johnson and *Kay, A Jay* by Christian Stevens.

SPEAKING AND LISTENING

TEACHERS NOTES

HAPPY HOUR

Objective: Listen to, learn and tell riddles and jokes.

Activities covered

- Evaluating jokes
- Explaining in own words why joke is funny
- Matching beginnings and endings of jokes
- Choosing a joke and telling it to a friend
- **Group work** – reading joke, voting for the best

Background information

This is a fun lesson and must be kept light-hearted and informal. Make sure that all jokes told by the children are appropriate.

Before the lesson

Children must be given a day or two's notice to bring to class their own short joke.

The teacher must have jokes ready to give each child (a selection follow).

The class will be divided into pairs and then groups.

The lesson (Pages 102 and 103)

The teacher reads through the copymaster to make sure children understand what is expected of them.

Children give a score out of 10 for the five jokes on the copymaster.

Children explain in their own words why a given joke is funny.

Children match the beginning and ending of five jokes.

Pair work – Children write their favourite joke and tell it to their partner. Their joke should not be one used in the lesson.

Group work – Each child reads his/her given joke and own joke to the group. Once all have been read, the group votes for the top three jokes.

The best jokes can be shared with the rest of the class.

Answers

1. Answers will vary.
2. The joke is funny because the boy misunderstood the teacher.
3. (a) Because he was a pain in the neck!
   (b) A cheetah!   (c) A monkey!
   (d) A chew-chew!   (e) Tell it a yolk!
4. Teacher check

Additional activities

Children can work out riddles.

Have a class discussion on funny scenes in well known films; for example, *Finding Nemo*, *Shrek*, *Sponge Bob Squarepants*.

Look at these websites:
www.squiglysplayhouse.com/JokesandRiddles
www.kieto.com/kids/kids_jokes.htm
www.humourmatters.com/kidsjokes.htm

Read funny poetry.

Collect *Doctor, Doctor!* jokes and create a class book.

Tell *Knock, knock!* jokes.

Jokes the teacher can give to the children:

Darren, at school dinner: I've just swallowed a bone!
Teacher: Are you choking?
Darren: No, I'm serious!

Patient: Doctor! Doctor! I keep hearing numbers instead of words!
Doctor: It must be something you eight!

Knock Knock
Who's there?
Lettuce
Lettuce who?
Lettuce in and we'll tell you.

What's the best thing to put into a pizza?
Your teeth!

What stays hot in the fridge?
Chilli sauce.

What did the sea say to the beach?
Nothing, it just waved.

Dad: Who broke the window?
Sam: It was Andrew, Dad. He ducked when I threw a stone at him.

Why were the elephants thrown out of the swimming pool?
They couldn't keep their trunks up.

What's a ghost's favourite game?
Hide and shriek.

What's as big as an elephant and weighs nothing?
An elephant's shadow.

Aunt: Do you ever help your little brother, James?
James: Yes, auntie, I helped him to spend the money you gave him yesterday.

What does a ghost do when he gets in a car?
Puts his sheet belt on!

Lady: I would like a pair of crocodile shoes please.
Assistant: Certainly, madam, what size is your crocodile?

What clothes does a house wear?
Address

What has a lot of keys but cannot open any doors?
A piano

What food do sea monsters eat?
Fish and ships.

What do you call a pig that does karate?
A pork chop.

What do you get if you cross a stream and a river?
Wet feet!

What falls but never gets hurt?
Snow!

What is a frog's favourite sweet?
A lollihop!

What does dirty rain do?
It showers.

What do you call a rich rabbit?
A million hare.

What do you call a fish with no eyes?
A fsh!

What biscuit flies?
A plain biscuit!

What do you call a sneezing sweet?
A chew!

Patient: Doctor! Doctor! I feel like a bucket!
Doctor: Yes, you do look a bit pail!

Why were the teacher's eyes crossed?
She couldn't control her pupils.

What bone will a dog never eat?
A trombone.

SPEAKING AND LISTENING

Silly stuff!

1) Some letters have been changed around in these sentences. What should these sentences be?

We are going to have some fun changing letters around. It won't always make sense!

(a) The tog wagged its dail.

(b) The sed is boft.

(c) The crince lost his prown.

(d) The can ate a make.

(e) The gorse jumped over the hate.

2) Change these sentences by changing the beginning letter of two words:

What a lunny fanguage!

(a) The boy climbed the tree.

(b) The teacher was cross.

(c) The little girl ate a pear.

(d) The puppy played with the ball.

(e) The lady drove the car.

SPEAKING AND LISTENING

Prim-Ed Publishing   www.prim-ed.com

Silly stuff!

3) In your group, write nonsense words that rhyme with these words. Read them!

ram	
root	
pen	
date	
fin	
seat	
sir	
nose	

4) Write two sentences with the letters mixed up. Your group must guess what they should be.

(a) _____

_____

(b) _____

_____

5) What was you favourite made-up word? _____

SPEAKING AND LISTENING

Happy hour

1) Read these jokes and give a score out of ten for each of them.

(a) **Q.** How do monsters like their eggs? /10
A. *Terror-fried!*

(b) **Q. Johnny:** I can't believe I just missed that goal. I could kick myself! /10
A. Jimmy: *Don't bother. You'd probably miss!*

(c) **Q.** What do you call a pig with three eyes? /10
A. *Piiig!*

(d) **Patient:** Doctor, Doctor! I feel like a pair of curtains. /10
Doctor: *Pull yourself together!*

(e) **Q.** What is a mermaid? /10
A. *A deep-she fish!*

2) Read this joke:

Gerry: Teacher, I'd like to bring my five dogs to school.

Teacher: But what about the noise and the mess?

Gerry: Oh, they won't mind.

(a) Do you think the joke is funny?   yes   no

(b) Explain why. _____

_____

SPEAKING AND LISTENING

Happy hour

3) Draw lines to match the jokes to their punchlines.

(a) Why did the little vampire have no friends?

(b) What animal do you have to watch out for when you write a test?

(c) What kind of key opens a banana?

(d) What do you call a toffee train?

(e) How do you make an egg laugh?

A chew-chew!

Because he was a pain in the neck!

A cheetah!

Tell it a yolk!

A monkey!

4) (a) Write your favourite joke here. _____

(b) Tell your joke to a friend.

(c) Did your friend laugh?

yes   no

Did you know?
On average, a 6-year-old will laugh about 200 times a day!

SPEAKING AND LISTENING

CLAP!

TEACHERS NOTES

Objective: Clap the rhythm of poems and rhymes.

Activities covered

- Clapping out names/words
- Writing words with a given number of syllables
- As a class – clapping rhyme
- Making up four-line poem, clapping it out

Background information

In this lesson, children have to clap to the syllables in the words. It is not necessary that the word 'syllable' be learnt but they should hear the word mentioned and know what it is.

Before the lesson

The teacher has ready examples of words to be clapped out as a class.

The lesson (Pages 106 and 107)

The teacher will give examples and, as a class, children will say how many syllables and clap the word out.

Children write their teacher's and their own name in full and clap them out.

Children clap out words given on the copymaster and write how many syllables.

Children clap out words and record words with 1/2/3/4 syllables.

As a class, children read aloud the given poem and clap it out. (To be read slowly!)

Children write their own four-line poem and clap it out.

This can be shared with the class.

Answers

1. Teacher check
2. puppy – 2, horse – 1, chicken – 2, frog – 1, porcupine – 3, bear – 1, butterfly – 3, crocodile – 3, sheep – 1, parrot – 2, rabbit – 2, lion – 2, zebra – 2, elephant – 3, hamster – 2, caterpillar – 4
3–6. Teacher check

Additional activities

Children can clap out short poems/rhymes; for example, *Nasty nursery rhymes* by Dave Calder, *The song of the engine* by H. Worsely-Benison and *We got rhythm* by Mike Jubb.

SPEAKING AND LISTENING

TEACHERS NOTES

THAT'S NONSENSE!

Objective: Listen to, read, learn, write and recite nonsense verse and rhymes.

Activities covered

- Reading a nonsense poem
- Underlining the nonsense words
- Rewriting the nonsense poem
- Writing nonsense rhyming words
- Changing a nursery rhyme

Background information

Children usually enjoy reading nonsense verse and there are many excellent nonsense poems available. This is meant to be a fun lesson, although children will be making full use of their phonetic skills! The poetry on the sheet is quite difficult; therefore, the answers should be completed as a whole class, with the teacher providing suggestions.

Before the lesson

The teacher can have ready examples of nonsense poems and rhymes.

The lesson (Pages 108 and 109)

As a class, children read the nonsense poem.

Children underline the words that do not make sense.

As a class, children rewrite the poem by adding real words to the poem instead of the nonsense words. The real words should rhyme with the nonsense words.

Children write rhyming nonsense words for the given words.

Children choose a nursery rhyme and write it.

Children change some of the words into nonsense words.

Children read their poem to the class who must guess what the original rhyme is.

Answers

1 – 4. Answers will vary, but a possible completed poem is:

> **A chance meeting**
>
> I went out walking one fine day,
> and met up with a cat.
> I stopped to greet him but he said,
> 'I haven't time to chat!'
>
> He looked a little thin and worn,
> I said, 'What's the rush about?'
> 'I'm looking for a house to rent,
> My master threw me out.'
>
> He said he hadn't munched in days,
> and was sleeping rough each night.
> The wild cats teased and bullied him,
> and tried to pick a fight.
>
> I thought about my comfy home,
> My soft and cosy bed,
> My kitchen full of food and snacks,
> 'Come live with me', I said.

5. Answers will vary. Examples:
   (a) gloop, noop
   (b) foodle, ploodle, quoodle
   (c) shink, bink, flink, glink, trink
6 – 8. Teacher check

Additional activities

Children can display their nonsense poems for the school to read.

Children can read other nonsense poetry; for example, poems by Spike Milligan or Edward Lear.

Children can make up their own nonsense verse.

SPEAKING AND LISTENING

Clap!

1 (a) Write your teacher's name and clap it out.

_____

A word is made up of syllables.

(b) Write your full name and clap it out.

_____

2 Clap out these words. Write how many syllables are in each word.

puppy ☐ horse ☐ chicken ☐ frog ☐

porcupine ☐ bear ☐ butterfly ☐ crocodile ☐

sheep ☐ parrot ☐ rabbit ☐ lion ☐

zebra ☐ elephant ☐ hamster ☐ caterpillar ☐

3 Write two words with one syllable.

(a) _____ (b) _____

Write two words with two syllables.

(c) _____ (d) _____

Write two words with three syllables.

(e) _____ (f) _____

4 Can you think of a word with four syllables? | yes | | no |

Write it here. _____

SPEAKING AND LISTENING

Prim-Ed Publishing   www.prim-ed.com

Clap!

5 As a class, clap out this poem.

Stew won't do

My Dad's favourite meal,
is home-cooked stew.
We all loathe it,
it's like eating goo.

Now, as far as stews go,
I think the idea's great,
a mish-mash of food,
piled up on your plate.

But instead of the vegies,
the lamb and the rice,
couldn't we create something,
tasty and nice?

A stew made of marshmallows,
chocolates and nuts,
would bring children running,
to sit on their butts.

At the dining room table,
they'd be asking for more.
And Dad's boring old dish
would have gone out the door.

6 Make up your own four-line poem about stew and clap it out!

_____

_____

_____

_____

That's nonsense!

1. Read the following nonsense poem:

You must talk nonsense in this lesson!

A flance sheeting

I went out nalking one fine day,
and met up with a jat.
I stopped to freet him but he said,
'I haven't time to kwat!'

He looked a little plin and forn,
I said, 'What's the nush about?'
'I'm dooking for a flouse to rent,
My plaster klew me out.'

He said he hadn't glunched in days,
and was fleeping rough each cnight.
The wild jats neezed and fullied him,
and tried to pick a snight.

I thought about my bumfy glome,
My soft and wozy smed,
My fitchen full of snood and klacks,
'Come chiv with me', I said.

2. Which words do not make sense? Underline them.

3. As a class, write possible words to replace the made-up words. Your words should rhyme with the nonsense words.

4. Rewrite the poem above, using your new words. Read the poem again.

SPEAKING AND LISTENING

That's nonsense!

5 Write nonsense words that rhyme with each of these:

(a) soup _____

(b) noodle _____

(c) think _____

6 Choose a nursery rhyme and write it (or just part of it) below.

The nursery rhyme
_____
_____
_____
_____
_____

7 Rewrite the nursery rhyme, changing some of the words.

Your nonsense rhyme
_____
_____
_____
_____
_____

8 Read your nonsense rhyme to your group/class.

Can they guess which rhyme it is?

yes   no

Prim-Ed Publishing   www.prim-ed.com

SPEAKING AND LISTENING   109

LISTEN!

TEACHERS NOTES

Objective: Recognise and recreate sounds in the environment.

Activities covered

- Writing down sounds children can hear
- Writing down sounds a person would hear in different environments
- As a class, making sounds
- Identifying children's own best and worst sounds
- **Pair work** – making and identifying sounds

Background information

This lesson makes children aware of the sounds and noises around them and gives them practice in recreating environmental sounds. It could be a noisy lesson!

Before the lesson

The teacher has ready ideas for different sounds in each of the mentioned places.

The class will be divided into pairs.

The lesson (Pages 112 and 113)

Children write down the sounds they can hear at that moment; for example, door closing, birds singing, chairs scraping, car.

Have a class discussion about the different sounds the children heard.

Children write down sounds they might hear in each of the given places. (Not the actual sounds, but descriptions of the sound; for example, trolleys scraping.)

Have another discussion about all the things the children wrote down.

The teacher mentions one place at a time, and one object. The class make the appropriate sound (noise) altogether; for example, the airport – a plane taking off.

Children write on the copymaster the sounds that were easy and hard to make.

Children write a list of sounds that they do and do not like.

Pair work – Children make sounds from their list. Their partner tries to guess the sound.

Answers

1. Teacher check
2. Answers will vary, but could include:
   (a) **Airport** – plane taking off and landing, loudspeakers, elevators, lifts, suitcases bring pulled, people crying, people laughing, buses, trucks, people walking, people talking
   (b) **Building site** – diggers, trucks, hammering, sawing, talking, drilling, trucks reversing, mixing concrete
   (c) **Supermarket** – people walking, trolleys squeaking, tills, announcements, talking, children crying (whining!), packing of shelves, tins falling down
   (d) **At playground** – swings, see-saw, children laughing, crying, shouting, running, crisp and sweet packets rattling, skateboarding, parents calling
   (e) **A farm** – cattle, sheep, pigs, tractor, farmer, chickens, dog barking, trucks, crows
3–7. Teacher check

Additional activities

Have a class vote for their favourite and their most irritating sounds. (Hopefully, the most irritating sound is not the teacher!)

Read poetry that has something to do with sounds; for example, *The sound collector* by Roger McGough.

Look at a website on noise pollution; for example:
www.cenyc.org/HTMLPE/noise.htm
(information for teacher).

SPEAKING AND LISTENING

TEACHERS NOTES

SOUNDS

Objective: Create real and imaginary sound worlds.

Activities covered

- Discussing sounds
- Writing where we might hear certain sounds
- Adding sounds to a haunted house picture
- **Group work** – planning and acting out a scene using sounds only

Background information

The lesson uses sounds and onomatopoeia to set a scene. Children will have to use their imagination as only sounds and sound words (and movement) are allowed.

Before the lesson

The teacher can have ready a list of various sounds, using school as an example perhaps; for example, Bang! Shh! Crunch! Ow!!! Mmm…, Crack!

The class will be divided into groups.

The lesson (Pages 114 and 115)

Have a class discussion on different sounds and where we might hear them.

Children write in the table where we might hear the mentioned sounds.

Children add sounds to a haunted house.

Group work – Children choose a scene, real or imaginary. They plan and sketch their scene, then act it out using sounds and movement only.

Once enough time has been given to practise, the group presents it to the class.

Discuss all scenes.

Answers

1. Answers will vary, but could include:
   glug – bath, sink, drinking **pop** – champagne bottle
   snap – breaking something **squeak** – door, mouse
   swish – horse's tail **crunch** – tyres on gravel
   crackle – fire **sizzle** – sausages in a pan
2. Answers will vary, but could include:
   Ah! Boo! creak, crunch, Eeek! squeak, snap, squish, Argh!, Shh!
3–5. Teacher check

Additional activities

Individual children or pairs can act out family scenes using sound only and the class must guess what they are doing.

Read poems about sound; for example, *What's that noise?* by Steve Turner and *Animal Form* by Kit Wright.

Where do children think is the quietest and noisiest spot in their school, their country, the world?

SPEAKING AND LISTENING

Listen!

1) Write down all the sounds you can hear right now.

The world is never a silent place!

_____
_____
_____
_____
_____
_____

2) Write down sounds you may hear in these places.

(a) airport _____
_____

(b) building site _____
_____

(c) supermarket _____
_____

(d) playground _____
_____

(e) farm _____
_____

3) As a class, practise making all the different sounds.

(a) Which sound was easiest to make? _____

(b) Which sound was hardest to make? _____

SPEAKING AND LISTENING

Listen!

4) Write a list of sounds you like.

- _____   • _____
- _____   • _____
- _____   • _____
- _____   • _____

5) Write a list of sounds you do not like.

- _____   • _____
- _____   • _____
- _____   • _____
- _____   • _____

6) Choose one sound you like. Make the sound.

Can your partner guess the sound?

yes   no

7) Choose one sound you do not like. Make the sound.

Can your partner guess the sound?

yes   no

Did you know?
The sound of someone snoring can be as loud as a pneumatic drill!

SPEAKING AND LISTENING

Sounds

The world is full of different sounds!

Did you know? Sound is measured in decibels.

1) Where might you hear these sounds?

glug	
pop	
snap	
squeak	
swish	
crunch	
crackle	
sizzle	

2) Add sounds around this picture to complete the scene.

114 SPEAKING AND LISTENING   Prim-Ed Publishing   www.prim-ed.com

Sounds

3) As a group, choose a real or imaginary scene such as in space, under the sea, the dinosaur world, a zoo—or choose your own.

(a) What is your scene? _____

(b) Write some sounds that will be heard in your scene.

- _____
- _____
- _____
- _____

- _____
- _____
- _____
- _____

(c) Draw your scene. Add sounds to your picture to complete it.

(d) Practise using these sounds and movement to depict your scene.

(e) Perform your scene to the class.

4) Did your class guess your scene correctly?

yes   no

5) Colour the stars to give your scene a mark out of five.

WHAT WOULD HAPPEN IF ...?

TEACHERS NOTES

Objective: Use imaginative play to create humorous characters and situations.

Activities covered

- Answering 'what if' questions
- Making up stories from pictures
- Group work – acting out scenes as given on copymaster
- Group work – planning and acting out scene from TV/film

Background information

Children must use role-play in this lesson without much rehearsal. Children must enjoy themselves in the lesson so tell them to keep it light-hearted and funny. Children will get the opportunity to tell their own funny stories to the class, which should get them thinking on the right lines.

Before the lesson

Optional – have ready more ideas for humorous situations.

The class will be divided into groups.

The lesson (Pages 118 and 119)

Have a class discussion about funny situations. Children can relate funny experiences they have had.

On the copymaster, children complete the 'what if' questions.

Children make up a funny story to go with each picture, saying what they think happened.

Group work – Children discuss their answers on the copymaster with the rest of the group. The group then acts out the scenes from Questions 1 and 2.

If there is time, various scenes can be presented to the class.

Group work – Brainstorm TV and film characters who are funny. Children write a list. Each group chooses one character and acts out a funny scene from the character's show. Children assess their performance.

Answers

Teacher check

Additional activities

Children can act out a familiar fairytale and change the story and characters as they go.

Children act out scenes between a headteacher and children, or between two animals such as a cat and a dog.

SPEAKING AND LISTENING

TEACHERS NOTES

READ THIS!

Objective: Engage with a wide variety of text, including informational material.

Activities covered

- **Pair work** – answering questions on timetable
- **Pair work** – having imaginary telephone conversation, making enquiries

Background information

This lesson focuses on children reading different types of text and comprehending it. There is such a variety of material that can be used here, the important aspect being that children are actively involved with reading the text and making sense out of it.

Before the lesson

The class will be divided into pairs.

Make a copy of the class timetable and give one out to each child for discussion.

The lesson (Pages 120 and 121)

Have a class discussion about the timetable. Ask questions such as, 'When do we do science?'/'What's the first lesson of the day on a Monday?'

Pair work – Children look at the timetable on the copymaster and answer basic questions.

Pair work – Children look at two cinema line-ups, and each chooses one.

Children have a telephone conversation making enquiries about the films showing.

Answers

1–2.
- (a) English
- (b) 3
- (c) Reading
- (d) English
- (e) Music
- (f) Maths
- (g) Assembly and Music
- (h) 5

3–4. Answers will vary, but could include:
What time is the show on Friday? Is the film *Cat and mouse* suitable for children? Can I buy popcorn? What is the cost of a ticket? What is the cinema's address? Do I have to book?

Additional activities

Children can look at graphs and bus or train timetables and answers questions and/or discuss.

Children look at picture books and see how the illustrations enhance the content.

Read poetry and discuss; for example, *The witch, the prince and the girl in the tower* by Sue Cowling (poem in a different shape).

Look at brochures of hotels/tourist spots near them.

Look at websites with children's reading. For example:
www.grimmfairytales.com and *www.childrenstory.com*

Prim-Ed Publishing   www.prim-ed.com

SPEAKING AND LISTENING

What would happen if ...?

1) Write what would happen if ...

(a) your trousers fell down at school?

_____

_____

_____

What would happen if you crossed a bug with the Easter rabbit? You'd get Bugs Bunny!

(b) you went to a party dressed up as a dinosaur, and it wasn't a fancy dress party?

_____

_____

(c) you pulled out a tin of beans at the shop and the whole pile came crashing down?

_____

_____

2) What do you think happened here?

(a)   (b)

_____   _____

_____   _____

_____   _____

3) Discuss your answers with your group. Choose one of the scenes from Questions 1 and 2. Act out the scene.

SPEAKING AND LISTENING

What would happen if ...?

4 Work as a group. Write a list of funny TV or film characters.

- _____   - _____
- _____   - _____
- _____   - _____
- _____   - _____

5 Choose one funny character.

Our character is _____.

In your group, practise a scene from this character's show.

Perform your scene for the class.

6 (a) Did your class think your scene was funny?   yes   no

(b) Which part of your scene was the funniest?

_____

_____

_____

(c) Colour the laughing faces to show how funny your scene was. (The more faces you colour, the funnier it was.)

Did you know?

Laughing is good for your health!

(d) How could you have made your scene funnier?

_____

_____

SPEAKING AND LISTENING

Read this!

1 Read this school timetable.

Monday			
Morning		**Afternoon**	
8.50 a.m. – 9.00 a.m.	Register	12.10 p.m. – 1.10 p.m.	Lunch
9.00 a.m. – 10.00 a.m.	Maths	1.10 p.m. – 1.30 p.m.	Reading
10.00 a.m. – 10.20 a.m.	Assembly	1.30 p.m. – 2.30 p.m.	Science
10.20 a.m. – 10.40 a.m.	Break	2.30 p.m. – 2.45 p.m.	Break
10.40 a.m. – 12.10 p.m.	English	2.45 p.m. – 3.30 p.m.	Music

2 With your partner, discuss and answer these questions about the timetable.

(a) What is the second lesson of the day?

_____

(b) How many breaks do they have?

_____

(c) What is the first lesson after lunch?

_____

(d) Which is the longest lesson?

_____

(e) What is the last lesson of the day?

_____

(f) What is the first lesson of the day?

_____

(g) When might the children sing?

_____ and _____.

Always read carefully!

(h) How many lessons are there on a Monday?

_____

120 SPEAKING AND LISTENING

Prim-Ed Publishing   www.prim-ed.com

Read this!

3 With your partner, read the following cinema advert.

GR8 CINEMAS

Snakeman 4
More action than ever before!
starring: SAM SNAKE and ANN ANACONDA
PG10
Now showing

The all new Cat and mouse
starring: ROD RODENT and KITTY KAT
Fun for the whole family!
ALL AGES

Shows: Monday to Friday 2 p.m., 6 p.m. Saturdays and Sundays midday, 4 p.m., 6 p.m., 10 p.m. **Address:** 34 Movie Street **Telephone:** 5556743
Tickets: £7.50
Booking essential on weekends. Sweets, snacks and drinks available.

---

4 (a) Choose one of the films each.

I have chosen _____.

(b) Write two questions you would like to ask the cinema about the film.

- _____

- _____

(c) Pretend your partner works at the cinema. Have an imaginary telephone conversation with your partner, asking questions about the film.

OLD FAVOURITES

TEACHERS NOTES

Objective: Respond to characters and events in nursery rhymes, books and films.

Activities covered

- Reading nursery rhyme
- Answering questions
- Writing description
- Giving description in oral form

Background information

The children must choose well-known stories or rhymes and take them further to think about what the characters may have been like if they were real. Characters in novels will obviously be more in-depth and complex than those in this lesson, but children can move onto these later.

Before the lesson

The class will be divided into groups.

The teacher can have ready some examples where characters can be discussed.

The lesson (Pages 124 and 125)

Have a class discussion about some nursery rhymes and the characters in them; for example, *Little Bo Peep* – What was she like? How did she lose her sheep? *Little Miss Muffet* – What was she like? (arachnophobic!) and so on.

Read the *Jack and Jill* nursery rhyme on the copymaster.

Children answer questions about the nursery rhyme and discuss their answers with the class.

Children write a description of a fictional character.

Children describe their fictional character to their group, who must guess who it is.

Answers

Teacher check

Additional activities

The class can discuss a well-known story; for example, *Goldilocks*. Discuss with the class what the characters may have been like – Daddy Bear, Mummy Bear, Baby Bear, Goldilocks.

In groups, children choose a fairytale and act out a scene from it, each person explaining who he/she is and what his/her character is like.

Read poems about different characters to the class; for example, *Mother Christmas's demand* by Andrea Shavick.

Read to the class some of Roald Dahl's *Revolting rhymes* – how are the characters the same/different from those in the original stories?

Children invent their own superhero/heroine, draw him/her and describe his/her character to the class.

Read well-known legends and fables to the children and discuss the characters in the story.

Children read stories on a website and describe the characters in the story; for example, www.storybookcastle.com

Children read the following poems and act them out:

Jack vs Jill

When Jack and Jill walked up the hill,
were they having a row?
Did Jill say, 'Jack, you hold the pail!'
And Jack say, 'No, not now!'

Did Jack and Jill then have some words?
Did Jill get really mad?
Did she think, 'I will get him back!
He's such a horrid lad!'

When they had made their bucket full,
and were on their way back,
Did Jill stick out her foot and say,
'Oh! Do be careful, Jack!'

Did Jack go tumbling down the slope,
and all because of Jill?
Did he hang on her ponytail,
and pull her down the hill?

A pail of water they had none,
and Jill began to cry.
'My crown got broke', said Prince Jack,
'and my bucket's dry!'

'So, stop your sniffling, let's go up,
cook needs water at ten.'
So Jack and Jill went up the hill,
but did they row again?

Friend or Foe?

I have a rare and special pet,
Pooky is his name.
Since he's come into my life,
it's never been the same.

We play together every day,
we talk for hours and hours.
I have to sneak him in the house
for him to have his showers.

See, Mum is not aware of him,
she doesn't know he's there.
She'd make me get rid of him,
and that would not be fair!

He's so concerned about my health,
he says I should eat more.
He says I should be so plump that
I won't fit through the door.

Yes, my friend cares a lot for me,
he says that he selects,
to be with me until the end,
My friend and pet T-Rex.

---

122 SPEAKING AND LISTENING

Prim-Ed Publishing www.prim-ed.com

TEACHERS NOTES

ABOUT YOUR BOOK

Objective: Engage frequently in informal discussion of books with the teacher and others.

Activities covered
- Answering questions as a group
- Looking at parts of a book
- Discussing book

Background information
This lesson involves talking about books. Although children have questions to answer, the questions are there to guide the discussion and make them look at their book more closely. Discussion within the group should be informal and relaxed. Teachers should have frequent discussions with the class about various books, such as the class reader. Talk about the author, the plot, whether they enjoy it or not, the publisher etc. Children must realise that there is a lot of information on the front cover, back cover, in the index and so on that can tell them more about the book itself.

Before the lesson (Pages 126 and 127)
The teacher must have ready different types of books to give to the groups; for example, a non-fiction book, a poetry book, a novel, an encyclopaedia, a picture book.

The class will be divided into groups.

The lesson
In groups, children discuss the book the teacher has handed to them.

The teacher reads through the page with the children to make sure that they understand all the questions. Show children the ISBN number, a table of contents, the copyright symbol. What are these used for?

Children answer the questions as a group and fill in their answers on the copymaster.

Groups swap books.

The same questions are answered for the rest of the books, but orally.

Answers
Teacher check

Additional activities
Children talk to a group about a book they have read.

The class can have a TOP 10 book list, based on class discussions of the best books they have read. This top 10 list must be reviewed and changed from time to time.

SPEAKING AND LISTENING

Old favourites

1) Read this well-known nursery rhyme and answer the questions.

> Jack and Jill went up the hill
> To fetch a pail of water.
> Jack fell down and broke his crown
> And Jill came tumbling after.

(a) Were Jack and Jill friends? _____

_____

(b) Why were they getting water? _____

_____

(c) How did Jack fall? _____

_____

(d) How badly was Jack injured? _____

_____

(e) Was Jill injured? How?

_____

_____

_____

2) Discuss your answers with the class.

Characters make a story!

124 SPEAKING AND LISTENING   Prim-Ed Publishing   www.prim-ed.com

Old favourites

3. Write a list of fantasy characters. For example: Barbie™, Spider-Man™, Winnie the Pooh.

4. Choose one fantasy character. Write his/her name.

_____

Did you know? Barbie™ was invented in 1959! How old is she now?

5. Write a description of the fantasy character, but do not mention his/her name.

_____
_____
_____
_____
_____
_____
_____
_____

6. Read your description to your group. They must guess who it is!

7. Did your group guess who your character was?   yes   no

About your book

Each group will receive a different type of book to study.

1) Answers these questions about your book, in your group.

What type of book is it? _____

What is the title? _____

Who is the author? _____

Who published the book? _____

Is it fact or fiction? _____

Does it look interesting? _____

Is the title catchy? _____

Does it have copyright? _____

Is the front cover exciting? _____

Does it have a table of contents? _____

Does it have an index? _____

What is the ISBN number? _____

How many pages are there? _____

Does it have illustrations? _____

Would you read it? _____

About your book

2 (a) Swap your book for a different book.

(b) Write the title of your new book.

_____
_____
_____

(c) Answer the questions again, but orally this time.

3 (a) Swap your book for a different book.

(b) Write the title of your new book.

_____
_____
_____

(c) Answer the questions again, but orally this time.

4 (a) Which was the easiest book for answering the questions?
_____

(b) Which was the hardest book for answering the questions?
_____

(c) Which question was the easiest to answer? _____
_____

(d) Why? _____
_____

(e) Which question was the hardest to answer?
_____
_____

(f) Why? _____
_____
_____

Did you know?
The most popular Dr Seuss books are Green eggs and ham *and* The cat in the hat.

WHAT EXPERIENCE DID YOU HAVE?

TEACHERS NOTES

Objective: Write about experiences – enjoyable/funny/annoying/frightening.

Activities covered

- Sorting experiences by type
- Writing about experiences
- Telling experience to the class
- Reading story
- Sorting experience

Background information

It is important to have an oral discussion before the children begin writing, to get the ideas flowing. Children are often keen to talk about their personal experiences – this lesson gets children to 'label', or sort, their experiences; for example, 'My experience was exciting and fun'.

Before the lesson

The teacher can give examples of experiences.

The lesson (Pages 130 and 131)

The teacher can give the class some examples of different experiences, perhaps discussing stories that are in the news, as long as they are not violent.

The teacher asks the class what kind of experiences we can have; for example, scary/nervous/sad/enjoyable/boring/frustrating/proud.

On their copymasters children write about different types of experiences they have had.

Children tell about their experience to the class and assess their talk. The class can then label the speaker's experience.

As a class, the teacher and children read through the story on the copymaster.

Children label Fred's experience.

Answers

1–4. Teacher check
5. Fred's experience was scary/unusual/frightening/unbelievable.

Additional activities

Children can write about everyday experiences; for example, visiting a relative, going to church, doing homework, playing sport.

Children read poems about other children's experiences.

SPEAKING AND LISTENING

TEACHERS NOTES

SENSE IT!

Objective: Draw and write about sensory experience – sight, hearing, taste, touch and smell.

Activities covered

- Answering questions
- Describing something using senses – written/oral
- Drawing pictures

Background information

This lesson concentrates on the senses and how we can express what our senses tell us. Obviously some things cannot be tasted, heard etc. – here the children must use their imagination.

Before the lesson

The teacher can have a selection of objects that can be described using the senses; for example, tins of food, spices, toys, pillow, wool, socks, bark, cutlery—anything!

The class will be divided into pairs.

The lesson (Pages 132 and 133)

As a class, the teacher discusses the objects he/she has brought in. Children must describe the various objects using the senses – What does it feel like? What does it look like? What does it sound like? What does it smell like? What does it taste like?

Children answer questions on their copymaster about what they can see/hear/taste/touch.

Children describe something using the senses, writing the description on their copymaster.

Pair work – Children read their description to their partner, who must guess what the object is.

Children draw pictures to describe things.

Answers

Teacher check

Additional activities

Children describe something using all their senses; for example, swimming in the sea.

Children can be blindfolded and, with a partner to guide them, explore the classroom or outside. The children should try to guess the things they are touching by using their other senses.

The website *www.littlegiraffes.com/fivesenses.html* contains ideas for teachers.

SPEAKING AND LISTENING

What experience did you have?

1) Write about an experience you have had that was ...

(a) enjoyable

(b) funny

(c) annoying

(d) frightening

2) Choose one of your experiences. Discuss your experience with the class.

It's good to share your experiences with others!

3) How well did you tell the class?

What experience did you have?

4) Read this story.

One day, there was a knock at the door. I don't usually answer the door to strangers, but my whole family was at home.

I expected to see the postman, or maybe a friend or one of Mum's friends. But no! Standing outside our front door was the greenest, ugliest creature I had ever seen. He had huge, bulging eyes and a long antenna that didn't seem to stop moving. I think he was trying to say something, but all that was coming out were sounds like 'zoink' and 'gloob', none of which were in my dictionary!

I just stood there, unable to move. I was trying hard to figure out whether he was dangerous or friendly.

'Who's at the door?' my mum shouted.

'Uh, I think it's an alien', I said.

"Oh, stop being so silly, Fred. Whoever it is, invite them in!' she replied.

'OK', said Fred.

5) Colour the words that describe the kind of experience Fred had.

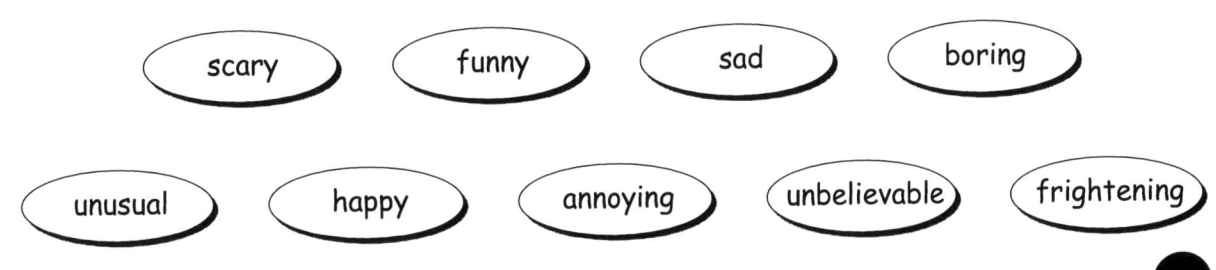

- scary
- funny
- sad
- boring
- unusual
- happy
- annoying
- unbelievable
- frightening

SPEAKING AND LISTENING

Sense it!

Have you lost your senses?

1) What are the five senses?

(a) _____

(b) _____ (c) _____

(d) _____ (e) _____

2) Write down eight things you can see now.

(a) _____ (b) _____

(c) _____ (d) _____

(e) _____ (f) _____

(g) _____ (h) _____

3) Write down six things you can hear.

(a) _____ (b) _____

(c) _____ (d) _____

(e) _____ (f) _____

4) What taste do you have in your mouth?

_____

5) Write down four things you are touching

(a) _____

(b) _____

(c) _____

(d) _____

Did you know? The human brain can remember about 50 000 smells!

SPEAKING AND LISTENING

Prim-Ed Publishing   www.prim-ed.com

Sense it!

6) Describe something using the senses.

What did you choose? _____

(a) What does it look like?	
(b) What does it sound like?	
(c) What does it feel like?	
(d) What does it taste like?	
(e) What does it smell like?	

7) Read your description to your partner. He/She must guess what it is!

8) Did your partner guess correctly? [yes] [no]

9) Draw pictures to describe the following.

What a car sounds like.

What ice-cream tastes like.

What cotton wool feels like.

MUSIC

TEACHERS NOTES

Objective: Listen to music and write about it.

Activities covered

- Listening to music
- Drawing pictures
- Discussing music

Background information

Children have varied tastes in music, often being influenced by what they have grown up with. This is a good opportunity to expose them to different types of music. Stress to children that they must be very quiet when listening to the music, and to close their eyes for full concentration. It is not necessary to play whole songs, excerpts will do if there is not enough time.

Before the lesson

The teacher must have ready different types of music to play to the children; for example, country, pop, classical, jazz, traditional Irish, opera.

The lesson (Pages 135 and 136)

Children listen to the four different types of music the teacher plays. Children must close their eyes and see what the music makes them think of.

The teacher plays the music again, and children must draw and write what the music makes them think of.

Children discuss their drawings with the class. Here, the teacher can play excerpts again to remind the children of the music.

Children listen to another type of music the teacher plays and answer the questions on their copymaster. Children discuss their answers with the class.

Answers

Teacher check

Additional activities

Children look at websites on music.

Children make their own musical instruments.

SPEAKING AND LISTENING

Music

1) Listen to the music the teacher is playing for you. Draw a picture for each piece of music and write what it reminds you of.

Music 1

What does it remind you of?

_____

Music 2

What does it remind you of?

_____

Music 3

What does it remind you of?

_____

Music 4

What does it remind you of?

_____

SPEAKING AND LISTENING

Music

2 As a class, discuss the different types of music you heard.

(a) Which music was your favourite?

_____

(b) How did the music make you feel?

_____

Music puts us in a mood!

3 Listen to the music the teacher is playing for you. Answer the questions.

(a) What type of music did your teacher play?

_____

(b) Did you like the music? yes no

(c) Why?/Why not? _____

_____

(d) How did the music make you feel? _____

_____

(e) What did the music remind you of? _____

_____

Did you know? Mozart started writing music when he was four!